# BEYOND THE COLD WAR

by Marshall D. Shulman

New Haven and London, Yale University Press, 1966

BEYOND THE COLD WAR

# Preface

THIS ESSAY is intended for readers who are not specialists in Soviet affairs. Its purpose is to contribute to the public discussion of policy issues by making available to such readers some of the information and insights which have resulted from the recent work of many scholars in this field.

Unlike new plays, which often have a "try-out" in New Haven and an official debut in New York, this book has traversed the route in the opposite direction. It was originally presented as a series of lectures before the Council on Foreign Relations in New York City during April 1965, and has since been revised and enlarged in response to the criticism of friends and colleagues who attended the lectures or reviewed the manuscript.

My list of indebtedness is embarrassingly disproportionate to the size of the book. The lecture series was sponsored by the Carnegie Endowment for International Peace, and the work of preparation was begun during a tour as Visiting Research Scholar at the Endowment during 1963–64. The completion of the work was made possible by a part-time appointment as Research Associate at the Russian Research Center at Harvard University.

To all these friends, colleagues, and institutions, I tender my grateful appreciation.

M. D. S.

*The Fletcher School of Law and Diplomacy*
*September 1965*

# Contents

# 1

# Retrospect

It HAS BECOME EVIDENT to most of us, I believe, that the language and ideas of the Cold War are no longer adequate as a guide to international politics today. For almost twenty years, the basic notions of the Cold War have dominated our thinking about world affairs, but these notions are in need of change. This is not because the conflict of purposes described by the Cold War no longer exists, but because this conflict is no longer the dominating fact of international politics and because the sources of this conflict have been changing. We are more than ready for some fresh conceptual approaches to deal with the complex currents which are now transforming the political world in unfamiliar ways.

On both sides of the Atlantic, there is a murmuring discontent with the prevailing philosophy of the Cold War, although no consensus has emerged as to what should take its place. This discontent is often part of the unarticulated background of policy differences within the Western alliance. Implicit in the discussion are varying assessments of the significance of recent dramatic changes in the Communist world, and some concern lest we cast away, out of weariness or a fascination for transient phenomena, what may still be valid and prudent in the prevailing Western outlook toward the Soviet Union.

In trying to decide to what extent our relations with the Soviet Union have changed, the first question we must deal with is: changed from what? We begin therefore with an effort to clarify our understanding of the past, with whatever detachment and insight the passage of two decades has placed at our command.

The matrix of the Cold War is to be found in the years 1945 to 1950. As we look back upon those years, briefly and quite schematically for our present purposes, they appear to us now as a spiral of interactions, tightening in a series of swift and convulsive stages.

The dominant impression one has, in thinking now about the early years of the Cold War, is how difficult it was, and still is, to separate what was real and what was distorted in the perception each side had of the intentions of the other. This is not to say that the conflict was a result of misunderstanding. The collision of incompatible interests was real, and extremely serious. But what powered the quick and violent intensification of the conflict into a clash of absolutes were the conditions within each country which affected its perception of the other. Each side,  for quite different reasons, developed oversimplified and emotionally colored stereotypes of the other, which obscured the real nature of the conflict. The result appears to have been a cycle of reactions that took on a life of their

own, disproportionate to and only partly related to the
real conflict of interest involved.

To disentangle the objective realities of those years
from the emotional exacerbating factors that prevailed
is still a contentious task, but it is both an intellectual and
a moral necessity, not for the purpose of assigning blame,
but to clarify our understanding of the real nature of the
conflict. To speak of "emotion recollected in tranquillity"
in the language of the poet may evoke a wry smile, considering how relative is our present tranquillity, but perhaps we are far enough from the events of those days to
speak of them with some detachment at least, and with
some retrospective insight into the underlying causes.

The two developments that appear to have dominated
the opening stage of the Cold War, in 1945 and 1946,
were the Soviet effort to consolidate its position in Eastern
Europe and the return of the Soviet leadership to those
attitudes of suspicion and hostility toward the West which
it had consistently and openly expressed before it entered
into the wartime alliance against Nazi Germany. Neither
development was sudden in its onset. The question of
Poland had of course been an issue at every wartime conference of the allies. The suspicion and hostility had been
manifested in some degree throughout the war, but with
increasing openness after the German defeat at Stalingrad
in the winter of 1943. By early 1946, Stalin had returned
to the language of ideological warfare and was projecting
a fifteen-year program of forced-draft concentration of
resources upon heavy industry and scientific research,
clearly reflecting an anticipation of possible war with his
recent Western allies.

The American reaction to these developments, as it unfolded in 1946 and 1947, compounded apprehension with feelings of guilt, anxiety, anger, frustration, and surprise. The surprise arose because of the illusions about the nature of the Soviet system that had been harbored and cultivated in this country before the Nazi–Soviet pact, during the war and for a while afterward. Undoubtedly it was mainly a matter of innocence, but many American liberals, politicians, and conservative businessmen alike had compromised their perception of totalitarian reality in the Soviet system, believing that this was a necessary concomitant to wartime cooperation and to mutual trust and collaboration in the postwar period. As might have been expected, this indiscriminate enthusiasm, being shallowly rooted, gave way to equally indiscriminate hatred, burning with a sense of betrayal and self-anger. There was guilt also because of the fate of Poland and the other states of Eastern Europe, sealed not at Yalta, but in the course of the war. A climate of anxiety had its roots in many causes: the atomic bomb, with its moral ambiguities and its awesome prospects; the trauma of the Hiss case upon an entire generation, the Fuchs case, the Canadian espionage revelations, and in time the paralyzing and degrading McCarthy episode. Anger and frustration and violence were in part an emotional hangover from the war and the self-brutalization it entailed; in part also they accompanied the turning of the tide in American politics, the long-repressed conservative reaction to twenty years of New Deal and wartime centralization. The slogan of "anti-Communism" itself became the American ideology.

Perhaps it would be unreasonable to have expected

an atmosphere of calm restraint in any case, but particularly so for the United States, whose major involvement in international politics had begun only after the First World War thirty years before, and whose people and institutions were unseasoned and sadly unprepared for the complexities and the burdens that were now their lot. The recent experience with Hitler Germany also was a complicating factor in several ways: there was a tendency to understand Soviet developments by analogy to German fascism, which was often misleading; and the record of liberal pacifism in its initial reactions to fascist aggression in the 'thirties had left residual confusions about the morality of force in international politics.

The effect of this emotional climate was to make clear perception and measured responses extremely difficult. In the face of this domestic turbulence, the record of governmental accomplishment seems the more remarkable. It would seem to be a fair judgment that the policy of containment, the Greek–Turkish Aid Program, the Marshall Plan, and the subsequent Berlin airlift and the organization of the Western alliance on the whole represented appropriate and reasonably successful reactions to the situation in Europe. In the space of two or three years, a revolution was accomplished in American foreign policy. A strong current toward withdrawal and demobilization was reversed; the United States was clearly committed to an international outlook and to the peacetime defense of Europe; an imaginative and unprecedentedly generous financial aid program amounting to almost thirty billion dollars was undertaken to restore European political and economic stability and to encourage the development of

European integration. The containment policy, especially in the form in which it came to be popularly understood, lacking the qualifications and subtleties of its original statement, evoked bitter and contradictory domestic resistance. Some of this resistance reflected the persistence of isolationism. Many had not yet accepted the reality of the conflict with the Soviet Union, or were reacting to the extreme terms in which the case against Soviet aggressiveness was being described. You may recall that a leading political commentator assailed the containment policy as a "strategic monstrosity," partly on the grounds of unfeasibility and partly because the ideological component of Soviet policy was not yet widely understood or accepted.

The measures that were intended by the United States to stabilize and protect Western Europe and the Eastern Mediterranean area appear to have been construed in Moscow within the framework of its preconceptions of the inherent aggressiveness of what it defined and stereotyped as "capitalist imperialism." For if it was emotional turbulence that distorted American popular perceptions, it was largely the ideologically shaped preconceptions of the Soviet leadership toward the outside world that were responsible for the primitive and distorted simplicity with which it interpreted the actions of the United States. These interpretations were in turn responsible for a reciprocal hardening of Soviet policies. It is by no means evident that the Soviet Union had begun its process of consolidation in Eastern Europe with a clear design in mind for proceeding toward the creation of what came to be called "Peoples' Democracies." A large degree of improvisation seems to have been involved, which represented not so much the opening of a new revolutionary advance in an immediate sense, but the securing of what were regarded as the fruits of victory, and the bulwarking of its security. However, given the Soviet ideologically distorted interpretation of the Truman Doctrine and the Marshall Plan as American efforts to challenge the Soviet position in Eastern Europe and to establish an American hegemony in Western Europe, the Soviet conception of security could allow for no stopping place short of total domination over Eastern Europe.

These interactions were related, both as cause and as effect, to the apparent emergence of a faction in Soviet politics led by Andrei Zhdanov, a narrow and dogmatic leader who tightened ideological lines of control at home and pressed for militancy abroad. In the justification of his policies, Zhdanov seized on each measure in the Western response as confirmation that Western intentions were aggressive and war was imminent. It cannot be proved, but his leadership under Stalin seems to have been responsible for the establishment of the Cominform, the further tightening of Soviet control in Eastern Europe, the coup in Czechoslovakia, the incitement of the Communist parties of France and Italy to undertake violently militant actions against their governments. Even more importantly, it was he who presided over the opening of the struggle for the control of Germany, which was to become the  most decisive territorial issue in the Cold War. With the blockade of Berlin and the airlift, cautiously opposing each other by measures short of war, the line that marked the westernmost advance of Soviet power into Central Europe was tested and held.

By the time of Zhdanov's death in late 1948, it had become apparent that Soviet misreading of events and miscalculations had resulted in a trend massively adverse to Soviet interests. Yugoslavia had been estranged, the Western zones of Germany were on the way toward unification, the militancy of French and Italian Communists had only served to contribute to the further cohesion and mobilization of the Western alliance. In the following years, the Soviet leadership sought to undo these consequences by intermittent gestures toward a reduction in the atmosphere of tension.

Once again, however, what now appears to have been a misreading of intentions on both sides was to carry tension to still higher levels. The Communist attack against South Korea, instead of being interpreted primarily in the local context of developments in Asia, came to be understood in the West, and I believe wrongly, as an indication of heightened Soviet militancy generally, which might also manifest itself by overt aggression in Europe and elsewhere. By the end of 1950, the Western mobilization was moving forward with a powerful momentum, driven by the conviction that the Soviet Union had both the capabilities and the intention of launching an attack on Western Europe as part of its program for military domination of the world. The United States reaction was colored and compounded, perhaps not wholly consciously, by two events which had immediately preceded the Korean War: the first Soviet nuclear explosion and the consummation of the Communist victory in China. These developments, plus the current preoccupation with espionage and the frustrations of fighting the first modern limited war, created a climate of legislative and public opinion of extraordinary intensity. In this climate, the United States administration found it possible to get legislative acceptance for higher levels of military appropriations which had originally been planned as a consequence of the Soviet nuclear explosion, but which had been shelved because of the costs involved.

In this climate, the administration also took the first steps toward the rearmament of West Germany. The effect was to complicate the internal political evolution of West Germany, to introduce serious political strains into the Western alliance, and to further freeze positions in Europe. Whatever possibilities may have existed for diplomatic adjustment of the German problem—and they may not have been substantial—were now further diminished. The effort to rearm the Federal Republic of Germany, thought necessary in the light of the imminent possibility of an overt military attack by the Soviet Union against Western Europe, in turn aroused a frenzied Soviet reaction, no doubt partly genuine and partly manipulative.

Of course it is difficult to say with certainty whether the prevailing Western picture of Soviet intentions was well founded or not. With the advantage of hindsight, however, and with no desire to impugn those who bore the responsibilities for our security, I believe that the impression of a planned Soviet military conquest of Western Europe was a misreading of Soviet intentions. There are many indications that Stalin fully appreciated the disastrous consequences of an overt move against Western Europe in the face of American strategic superiority. Moreover, although the Soviet Union made use of its considerable strength in France and Italy for political action against these governments, and for clandestine operations in the event of war, Stalin was not prepared to encourage the French and Italian Communist parties to seize power, although the militant wing of the French party had wished to do exactly that.

It should be added, however, that all we know about Soviet behavior in this period suggests that had there been no risk in further expansion, and no effective resistance, in all probability Soviet probing would have been far less conservative than it was. The organization of the Western defense and the American commitment to that defense were necessary to restore the confidence and political stability of Western Europe, and to ensure against any temptation of a militant Soviet leadership to consider that a military attack could be successful. What is at issue is a question of degree, of proportion, of emphasis. By overestimating the threat of Soviet military conquest, we were led to override political considerations in the face of what we believed to be the higher military priorities.

Another factor that made judgment difficult at that time was the deployment of the large Soviet land army to move quickly into Western Europe in the event of an American nuclear attack. "There is an element of tragic irony [I am quoting a few sentences from something I wrote several years ago] in the way in which Soviet superiority in armed forces and Western superiority in nuclear weapons, instead of creating a military equilibrium in this period, led to an interacting spiral of mutual anxiety and rearmament. . . . The irony is heightened by the fact that the means chosen by the Soviet to compensate for its sense of vulnerability stimulated Western military mobilization."

The spiral of armaments, while clearly not a cause of the Cold War, became, like the interaction of distorted perceptions, a complicating and intensifying factor. Each side felt a sense of vulnerability, which was heightened by the efforts of the other to overcome its corresponding feeling. Even before the war had ended, the Soviet leadership had begun to concentrate its resources on the earliest possible development of a modern military technology, to overcome the acute vulnerability it felt in the face of United States strategic air and nuclear power. Meanwhile, by the deployment of its land army, and by a foreign policy that used both tension and the easement of tension, the Soviet Union sought to deter the West from using, or gaining political advantage from, its nuclear strength before Soviet science could break the Western monopoly.

By the middle 'fifties, Stalin's successors harvested the fruits of his concentration of resources on the development of jet bombers, nuclear weapons, and missile delivery systems, and the strategic military relationship began to change its character. No longer was it a matter of Western nuclear preponderance versus Soviet preponderance in conventional land forces. The appearance of Soviet jet bombers was followed by intermediate range and then intercontinental range missiles; the Soviet atomic bomb by the Soviet hydrogen bomb. It was undoubtedly the expectation of the Soviet leadership that the acquisition of these weapons would produce what was optimistically called "a shift in the balance of power," which was expected to yield substantial political advantages. As the arsenals increased, however, the sense of vulnerability deepened because of the nature of the weapons themselves, which favor the offense over the defense, and also because of overestimations of what the other side was up to. The "bomber gap," the "missile gap," and the presumed "conventional gap" all reflected the prudent concern of men responsible for particular sectors of the defense of their country. The net effect of this aggregate of prudence, however, was the continued upward climb of the world's potential for violent destruction, and the price of equilibrium.

But the fact is that an equilibrium of sorts did emerge. The dominant characteristic of the Cold War over the past decade has been a tendency toward the acceptance of a certain strategic stabilization as between the United States and the Soviet Union. Mutual vulnerability has had the practical political effect of creating a gross parity, a condition of mutual deterrence that is not sensitive to relatively large inequalities in particular categories of weapons. The armament competition, although still very large, has not proceeded at anything like maximum capability on either side. The Soviet Union, contrary to American fears and expectations, did not go into maximum mass production of its intercontinental missiles. Each side has appeared to accept the fact that the other is fully aware of the damage that would result from a nuclear war, however initiated, and the expectation of strategic nuclear war in the near future appears to be low on both sides. Each has tended to accept certain tacit restraints in the interest of avoiding gross disturbances to the strategic stability— with the important exception of the Cuban episode. The fact that less than three years have elapsed since the Cuban experience, and that the condition of mutual deterrence could be upset by miscalculation, by third-party action, by irrationality, or by radical technological developments, creates some uncertainty about the durability of this condition. On the other hand, this degree of stabilization has been furthered by the protection given to retaliatory forces, by the absence of any great technological advances in defense against missiles, and by the recent tendency in military planning to consider the most probable dangers rather than to prepare for the worst imaginable contingencies.

This strategic stabilization has had in turn a number of profound consequences in the political dimensions of the Cold War.

*First*—Within the alliances on each side, the recognition by the two powers of the inhibiting effect of mutual vulnerability and the destructiveness of modern war has released fragmenting tendencies. Within the Communist group of nations, the stabilization has of course been a major complicating factor in China's challenge to Soviet leadership. Within the Western alliance, the fragmenting process is stimulated by a confusion between military stabilization and political détente.

*Second*—The strategic stabilization has given greater emphasis to the political uses of military capabilities, which become more important as the possibility of their actual employment in war diminishes.

*Third*—The European theater of the Cold War, both East and West Europe, has become a field of primarily political and economic maneuver, competing for shifts of

orientation in the opposing camps within relatively narrow limits.

*Fourth*—The field of broader action has shifted to the
underdeveloped areas, where the same inhibitions do not
extend to lower levels of violence.

*Fifth*—The strategic stabilization has resulted in greater emphasis by the Soviet leadership upon the repair and
development of the Soviet economy as a key factor in the
further expansion of Soviet power and influence.

Each of these developments will require more detailed
attention at a later point, but what is relevant here is that,
partly as a consequence of the strategic stabilization (together with several contributing factors to be discussed),
the conflict relationship between the Soviet Union and the
West has passed from a stark postwar confrontation to a
more ambiguous stage in which the balance of conflicting
and parallel interests is less clearly defined, and the conflict itself has a more diffuse character.

Our brief retrospective review began with the question:
changed from what? I have suggested that the postwar
stage of the Cold War can best be understood by trying
to separate the underlying causes of conflict from the
secondary intensifying factors. In identifying the prime
causes of conflict, the record seems fairly clear. Although
the United States was certainly not without fault, it is
disproportionate to argue, as some writers have done, that
the abruptness of the cancellation of the Lend-Lease arrangements with the Soviet Union, the mishandling of the
Soviet loan request, the severity of President Truman's
reception of Soviet Foreign Minister Molotov en route
to the founding meeting of the United Nations, or other

conclusion

instances of United States ineptitude or inconsistency as the war drew to a close, were of a sufficient order to have created a legitimate basis of Soviet concern for its security against a Western attack. Had the United States conducted war operations with a consciousness of postwar political effects, had the United States put more reliance on power and less on idealistic declarations of principles, had the people of the United States been more aware of history and less subject to superficial and blinding enthusiasms, there might have remained legitimate grounds for doubt whether a more open and trusting policy would not have moved the Soviet leadership to find its own self-interest in somewhat greater cooperation. As it was, the virtue of these shortcomings was in making it clear in retrospect that the initial Soviet actions in the Cold War cannot be sufficiently explained as defensive reactions to a Western challenge. Perhaps the tragedy was that the particular leaders then in command of Soviet policy were men disposed toward a narrowly dogmatic outlook; whether the system could have provided alternative leadership tendencies at that time is of course a matter of purest speculation. As it was, however, and with all the allowance one can make for possible national bias, I believe we must give central place in the assignment of prime causes of the Cold War to the combination of the Soviet effort to improve its national power position in the disordered condition of the postwar world and the ideological perceptions and expectations of the Communist leadership.

In speaking of the influence of ideology on Soviet behavior, it seems useful to identify the particular functions it has performed. Chief among these functions has been the ideological influence on Communist perceptions of non-Communist systems as inherently and intractably hostile, with the consequent conviction that conflict at some level was inevitable. The companion of this perception has been the fundamental expectation of Soviet ideology regarding the future course of history: that non-Communist societies were fated to collapse and be succeeded by societies molded on the Soviet pattern. It has been this component of the Soviet outlook that has made Soviet dynamism more complex and less susceptible to territorial stabilization than if it simply reflected the bursting energy of a nation-state entering upon a virile stage of development.

I think we are obliged to recognize, however, that this Soviet commitment to the ultimate worldwide ascendancy of Communism became vulgarized in the prevailing Western stereotypes as a more immediate, unlimited, and primitive conception of world revolution in a near and military sense. Perhaps democratic societies cannot be galvanized sufficiently by measured intellectual analysis, and perhaps the strengthening of Western power—which was absolutely essential—could not have been accomplished without the adrenalin of great anxiety, but it is nevertheless useful for us to appreciate to what degree our own perceptions and responses had a reciprocal, exacerbating effect upon the conflict itself. As we have seen, our understanding of the real dimensions of the conflict was distorted, leading us to give disproportionate responses to the military challenge, and too narrow a response to the political requirements of the period, requirements that arose from other causes than the Soviet challenge alone.

As the Cold War moved out of its first postwar phase, some of these secondary factors of intensification have subsided. During periods when tension has abated, there is in fact a tendency for the simplifications of the first stage to yield to their opposites, which minimize the conflict of purposes still remaining. When tension is renewed, however, the emotion-laden stereotypes of pure hostility tend to return. Our present necessity is to clarify public understanding of processes which are by nature ambiguous and in transition, in order that we may be capable of judgments involving differentiations of degree rather than fluctuations between simplified extremes.

# 2

# The Changing Terrain of International Politics

LET US TURN now to another thread in the argument. It is sometimes misleading, I believe, to deal with the Cold War as an encapsulated problem, to focus attention too narrowly upon the esoteric developments of the Communist world as detached from the underlying forces of international politics. The whole terrain of international politics has been radically transformed since the end of the war, and it is illuminating to begin with this fact and to trace from the source some of the forces that have been inducing change not only in the Soviet system and policies but in our own as well.

It is not the revolution of Marx and Lenin that is transforming the world, but the radical effects of modern military technology; the new forms and uses of energy in nonmilitary technology, such as transportation and communications; the continued upsurge of industrial techniques in the already industrial areas, with profound consequences for their societies; and the explosive force of nationalism in the former colonial areas and, to some extent, in the industrial parts of the world as well. These are all more or less familiar phenomena, and it has become a commonplace to speak of them as "the revolutions of our time," but we are in truth a long way from having absorbed the implications of these transformations into our analysis of international politics and even less so into our policies. As a step in this direction, let us reflect for a few moments on some of the ways in which these factors have been affecting the conditions within which the Cold War has been evolving.

To begin with, it seems evident that the radical increase in the destructiveness and cost of modern weapons has had a curious paradoxical effect upon the configuration of power in the world, and has even called into question our familiar conceptions about the very nature of national power. In the current debate about whether we have moved from a bipolar world toward some multipolar configuration of power, the paradox is especially evident in the confusion of the different senses in which the notion of national power is applied. If we are thinking of the power to wage a large-scale nuclear war, the world is still in a fundamentally bipolar situation, and seems likely to remain so for some time to come. Even if a number of other countries develop the capacity to discharge some nuclear weapons, sufficient to carry out local nuclear military operations or to trigger a larger war, only two nations have the resources sufficient to conduct a strategic nuclear war. On the other hand, if we consider the inhibitions against the use of strategic nuclear weapons, so dispropor-

tionate to most political purposes, it is apparent that many
nations (not only the medium powers, but small as well)
have indeed become multiple poles in the distribution of
other forms of power—power to influence the course of
events through small wars, through economic and political strength, ideas, diplomatic energy, and even, on occasion, through statesmanship.

In this sense—that is, apart from the conditions of
general war or extreme tension—the significant design in
international politics is not bilateral but polygonal. In
the shade of the nuclear umbrella, varieties of alignment
and demi-alignment have flourished. It is no longer possible to think in unitary terms of broad categories of nations or of continental groups of nations, in simplifying
the design of international politics. Significant subgroup-
ings within the Soviet bloc, the Western alliance, and the
"third world" require such a variety of cross-hatchings on
a political map as would tax the ingenuity of a map-
maker. What is implied in this variegated cross-hatching
is a growing international acceptance of degrees of allegiance and a certain flexibility in political action outside
the alliance systems.

The effect upon the Cold War has been to create a
certain schizotic confusion about the various levels of conflict that dominate the forefront of our consciousness at
various times. Much of the time we are preoccupied with
lower levels of political, economic, or guerrilla conflict
within a loose polygonal structure, but on occasion we
find ourselves reminded that the gross bipolar structure
in the background is still ultimately significant because of
the potential consequences of a general nuclear war.

In the ambiguous twilight zone of potential nuclear war, we become aware how much the developments in military technology have been changing the relationship between war and politics, and how greatly this has affected the evolution of the Cold War. For a nation committed to a process of change, the realization that modern large-scale war cannot be a continuation of politics is a difficult one to absorb even if it has no deliberate intention of launching an attack, since the stabilization of the military environment tends to create a certain détente in the political realm as well, and a constraint on political action. This condition has been one of the forces working toward the attenuation of the revolutionary impulse in Soviet policy. Another consequence of this realization has been an increasing Soviet attention to other instrumentalities, especially economic power, as levers for achieving the ultimate transformations to which the Soviet ideology is committed. Along with this goes an increasing concern for the *political effects* of weapons systems, as distinguished from their putative usefulness in the actual event of war—that is, a choice of weapons systems in part at least based upon the effect they are thought to have upon political behavior. The Soviet Union has been more consistently conscious than the United States of the role of force as a backdrop to international politics, and this concern for the peacetime political utility of weapons has been one factor that has made the introduction of arms control measures more difficult.

On a few vivid occasions, the Soviet Union and the United States have found themselves drawn into playing a kind of poker game test of will around a crisis point, in the twilight zone where the implied willingness to use nuclear weapons is a marginal form of diplomatic pressure. Sober afterthoughts about the risks that pure chance and possible miscalculation may introduce into such encounters have created transient periods of receptivity for safeguards against inadvertent war, but the political imagination has not been retentive enough, and the minatory image has faded before substantial safeguards could gain acceptance.

This leads us directly to consider a related effect of the transformation in military technology—the way in which changing conceptions of security have had a bearing upon the evolution of the Cold War. The primary paradox here has grown out of the fact that the tenuous security of mutual deterrence has emerged out of the universal increase in vulnerability to total destruction. In Chapter 1 we have already touched upon some of the consequences for the Cold War of this strategic balance, and we will be returning to the subject once again later when we come to a discussion of arms control, but it is worth reminding ourselves at this point that there are many reasons for regarding the present strategic stabilization as a temporary lull rather than as a long-term basis for security. One of the reasons for this is the uncertain effect of future technological change upon the weapons equilibrium. Many scientists believe that there do not appear to be on the near horizon many great scientific leaps like those that made their appearance during the war and in the early postwar years, but that wider application of presently available science to military technology could make the situation ten years from now as different from the present as the present is from the situation ten years ago—that is, before the age of missiles. The rate at which science is applied to military technology, however, depends somewhat on the level of tension, since these measures are extremely costly, and the incentives appear to be chiefly negative—that is, the desire not to be without something the other side may be developing.

This prospect of qualitative leaps in the arms competition as the result of such potential technological developments as an antiballistic missile system, together with the risks of miscalculation around crisis points, the apparent probability of the spread of nuclear weapons, and the possibility of the enlargement of local wars—all raise the urgent question whether the present plateau of strategic stabilization can long remain a sufficient security against nuclear war, without being underpinned by safeguards against these specific hazards. This question is more fully examined in the last chapter, but the point that is relevant here is that the strategic stabilization, however temporary it may turn out to be, has already had a qualitative effect upon the Cold War. The arms race has taken on a dual character. One of its aspects is marked by deadly competition for advantages that may be decisive in case of war, or may be vital in the political conflict. The other aspect reflects the interests that the adversaries have in common against the factors that tend to increase the danger of inadvertent war. Perhaps it is more accurate to speak of overlapping interests than mutual interests, but each side has slowly begun to accept the realization that more military power does not always produce more security, that there is an interacting process at work between the adversaries, and that in an ultimate sense the security of each side is interlocked with that of the other. The result has been a gradual acceptance of certain restraints in practice, and a certain amount of guarded communication between adversaries. Although they appear to be contradictory in their effect, both aspects are part of the present reality, and the coexistence of these conflicting conceptions is perhaps the major change in the situation as contrasted with, say, fifteen years ago. The question posed by these dual aspects of the military confrontation is whether it will be possible to find ways of introducing safeguards into the arms race without sacrificing the political interests of those who are still fundamentally adversaries. I believe it *is* possible, as I shall try to show later on.

Outside the military field, other technological applications have also been exerting a transforming effect upon international politics and the Cold War. This is a subject that will bear much further study, but it is obvious when we stop to think of it that advances over the past twenty years, particularly in transportation and communications, have been changing both the mechanics and the substance of diplomacy perhaps more than most of us have realized. Some of these changes affect the general environment of international politics, and a few are directly relevant to the evolution of the Cold War.

One of the most striking effects of advances in transportation and communications upon the conduct of diplomacy is the extent to which the command and control of foreign policy have become increasingly centralized. The consul on the spot has become a lesser adjunct of the console of communications before the head of state and his foreign office. That it is now possible for a chief executive to take direct responsibility for day-to-day developments in remote places, or to send personal envoys overnight anywhere in the world, or to engage in frequent "summitry" by jet or by television with friends or adversaries—all these technical possibilities have tended to transfer to the machinery and the top leadership at home many of the details of foreign policy management. Moreover, the line between domestic and foreign policies has become less distinct as world developments are impressed vividly and even insistently upon both leaders and the public, and it has become increasingly difficult for the leadership of any major nation to keep foreign issues in the background, even when it wishes to do so.

The pace and immediacy of diplomatic activity have also been affected. Time and distance once cushioned remote encounters; today the major capitals are directly involved with each other within a matter of hours over developments anywhere in the world. Diplomatic reaction times to events in areas formerly remote are now virtually instantaneous—faster sometimes than the speed of thought. Policies change more quickly, and interact much faster, so that the alternations in the climate of the Cold War, which once could be charted in periods of several years at a time, must now be measured from month to month.

Also, the area of encounter has become worldwide. Contiguity has become a diminishing factor in defining areas of contact and conflict. Hardly a problem anywhere remains local in character or escapes involvement in

global politics. Such traditional political-geographic con-
cepts as "buffer zones" and "lines of communication" have
been losing some of their significance. As a consequence,
traditional diplomatic techniques for reducing tension by
easing points of peripheral contact or for encouraging
stability by a physical separation of "zones of influence"
have become less meaningful than they once were, particularly in the advanced industrial areas.

Another consequence of geographical mobility is that
the reach of organized political activity has been extended.
Demonstrations have been synchronized in a dozen places
around the world to respond to events the day before. For
better or for worse, apparently limitless possibilities have
unfolded for the propagation of slogans, propaganda,
ideas, and information into every rice paddy and jungle
clearing. But the substance as well as the techniques of
international politics have been affected as travel and
various forms of communication across cultures and conti-
nents have multiplied. Inevitably, as more people have
had some form of direct contact with other countries, the
effect has been to reduce the "foreign" quality of other
cultures and systems. The diffusion of cultural patterns,
social values, political institutions, and even popular fads
has been markedly accelerated. For totalitarian societies,
it has become increasingly difficult to close off a population from foreign influences or to rely upon secrecy as a
source of security. To a significant degree, Soviet institutions have had to be adapted to the irresistible flow of
information to and from the rest of the world. The historical Russian isolation from foreign influences was in
part at least a result of difficulty in travel; today, police
techniques may impede but they cannot indefinitely hold

off the reduction of this isolation by modern technology, particularly if the political leadership regards the flow of information as a necessary concomitant to the industrial development of the country.

We have touched upon only a few of the ways in which technology has been affecting international politics, and once the mind turns in this direction innumerable illustrations begin to present themselves. But if we ask ourselves what, in gross terms, the dominant effect of changing non-military technology has been upon the Cold War, perhaps the answer would be that it has stimulated the shift of focus from Europe to the underdeveloped areas. On the one hand, technology has contributed to the stabilization of the European theater of the Cold War by providing the technical underpinning of integration, and by narrowing the logistic distance between Europe and the United States. On the other hand, technology has made the under-developed areas more readily accessible as a theater of competition in the Cold War, not only to the Soviet Union and the Western countries, but also to China. There are other reasons for this shift of focus, some of which we will come to in a moment, but technology is certainly an important contributory factor.

A related factor of change in international politics has been the phenomenal and unanticipated further growth of the advanced industrial areas—particularly in Western Europe and Japan—partly as a result of government policies favoring investment and growth, and in part the effect of an extraordinary continuing increase in productivity through the application of modern technology, some of it borrowed from the United States. One major consequence of this development has been the return of Europe to a greater prominence in international politics.

Much has been written about the effect of the high growth rate in Western Europe in stimulating what has sometimes been called "a search for identity" and sometimes "a new nationalism," and I shall with difficulty limit myself here to a brief enumeration of a few consequences of this development that may be immediately relevant to our purposes.

It is apparent that the weakening of the Western alliance as a result of the growth of European self-confidence and self-reliance has raised the possibility of a new major economic and political power center in the world, whose degree of association with, or opposition to, American power is a principal determining question for the immediate future. As we shall see, this development has been an important factor in the evolution of Soviet policy. The rise of Europe has also raised the thorny question of nuclear proliferation, which lies at the heart of the thrust for European self-reliance, for the ambiguity of the nature of national power in the present period to which we referred earlier leaves it unclear whether the power to exert a major influence in world affairs can only be based upon an independent strategic nuclear capability. This issue too has exerted a shaping influence on Soviet foreign policy.

Also, the rate of growth in Western Europe and in the other advanced industrial countries has further widened the gap between themselves and the underdeveloped areas, with possibilities for exacerbating future conflicts between these two parts of the world.

Further, the European (and Japanese) growth rates

have been a fundamental contradiction of the Marxist–Leninist expectations concerning the decline of capitalism. Moreover, the social and political consequences of this economic growth have been inhospitable to proletarian revolutionary dynamism. High growth rates have weakened the class struggle and encouraged the spread of a middle-class outlook in European societies. What some writers have referred to as "the decline of ideology" at least in the revolutionary sense of ideology, has been reflected in the movement of European socialism in the direction of non-Marxist reformism, and even of the Communist parties of Italy and France toward conservative operation within the existing political and social system.

What the long-term effects of this advancing industrialization are likely to be upon the social and political organization of modern societies—the Soviet as well as Western—has been the subject of an interesting literature; such questions have been explored as whether industrialization is inevitably accompanied by pluralist trends, or trends toward technocracy and bureaucratism, and whether such trends will moderate Soviet totalitarianism and conversely will increase centralization in Western political systems. Fascinating as it is, this range of questions leads outside our present framework, but we will want to follow it along at least a little way when we come to discuss the evolution of Soviet society.

Finally, among the factors in international politics that have been changing the external environment have been of course the rapid decolonization in Asia and Africa and the explosion of nationalism throughout the underdeveloped world. The swiftness and lack of preparation with which the four-century-old European colonial system was liquidated has left a legacy of turbulent upheaval that now appears destined to dominate international politics for some time to come.

The many new nations which have been formed, once described as a "third world" in international politics, have been prevented from functioning as a unitary bloc by intense ethnic, religious, tribal, and nationalist conflicts, as well as by their involvement in the broader currents of international politics. In some areas, the disintegrative phase of nationalism appears to be yielding to regional economic and political groupings, perhaps foreshadowing the next phase in this development. The political life of the United Nations, still congested by the sudden enlargement of its membership, is just beginning to reflect the sorting-out of the new regional groupings.

The major complicating factor in the upheavals throughout the underdeveloped world has been the rise of China as an independent power, with its radical revolutionary involvement throughout Asia, Africa, and Latin America. The responsiveness of some revolutionary cadres in these areas to the dynamism of the Chinese appeal seems to have become the major inhibiting factor operating against trends toward moderation in Soviet policy. Economic development in these areas has for the most part been slower and more difficult than was optimistically forecast a few years ago (recall the optimism with which the "Point Four" program was launched), often not keeping up with population growth, and the widening gap between the "haves" and "have-nots," stirred by venomous and irrational resentments against the West, darkened by ominous racial overtones, has in it the potentiality of making the coming decade in international politics one of continuing violence.

These are in brief some of the forces that have been at work transforming the terrain of international politics in recent years. The value of beginning with these conditions in considering the evolution of the Cold War is that it increases our sensitivity to the *process of adaptation* to the external environment which is often overlooked in the study of Soviet policy. This process—partly conscious and partly unintended—by which the Soviet leadership seeks to make its efforts effective under changing conditions, has had a transforming effect upon Soviet policies and the Soviet system, and has been an important factor in opening up the dispute with the Chinese.

Before we go on to analyze how this has operated, there is one general observation I should like to make about the developments we have been discussing. The main impression that emerges from this perspective is how much the Cold War has lost its centrality. Whereas in its first postwar phase the confrontation between the Soviet Union and the United States was the dominating fact of international politics, and of internal politics in both countries, today this confrontation no longer holds the center of the stage. The conflict of purposes between these two systems has become caught up in the turbulent currents of international politics.

It is no longer sufficient—if indeed it ever was—for the leaders of either country to define their policies simply by reference to the other. These countries are like two tired wrestlers whose ring is swirling with many former spectators, and whose bout has become something of a free-for-all. The attention of the leaders of both countries is less narrowly focused upon the other. The first decade of the Cold War, as we have seen, was chiefly characterized by the redefinition of power lines in Europe and by the development of stability in Western Europe as well as some measure of stability in the strategic military relations between the United States and the Soviet Union. We have now passed into a stage whose main characteristic appears to be a differentiation between the limited field of maneuver in the still decisive but largely stabilized European theater, and the trackless movement of revolutionary conflict in the underdeveloped areas, complicated by the Chinese effort to establish its influence by militant policies.

If this is true, it is evident that old habits of thought, rooted in the simplified drama of the early years of the Cold War, will not lead to adequate responses to the kinds of problems that now confront us.

# 3

# Transformations in the Soviet System

IN DEALING WITH A DISTANT SOCIETY, we sometimes permit ourselves to reduce things to manageable simplifications which we would hesitate to accept in dealing with the jumble of detail closer at home. This phenomenon has been particularly apparent among the ventures of some foreign observers into quite sweeping generalizations about trends in Soviet society.

We need, of course, to try to form some notions, however tentative, about what is happening to the Soviet system, for both intellectual and practical reasons. The evolution of the Soviet social structure, under conditions that illustrate the interaction of modern totalitarianism and advancing industrialization, represents an intriguing contribution to the comparative study of contemporary political and social development. On the practical side, there is the obvious linkage between Soviet internal developments and the dynamism of Soviet foreign policy.

The range of Western speculative responses to these

questions has been broad and far from unanimous. Some writers have seen recent developments as part of a process of liberalization; others emphasize the continuing dominance of the Communist Party. Some stress the rapidity of social change; others say such changes are but superficial and that fundamental transformations are proceeding at a glacial pace. Many observers are attracted by the notion of the rise of a "managerial class" in the Soviet Union and, with it, the replacement of revolutionary ideology by pragmatic problem-solving. A companion of this view—mildly Marxist in perspective—is what has come to be called the "fat-man thesis," that Soviet society is becoming and must necessarily become more conservative as it reaches a higher level of economic development. Others, to balance the picture, see economic development as leading to a depersonalized technocratic dictatorship, no less dynamic in its foreign policies.

For our present purpose, which is to consider the relationship between transformations in the Soviet system and the evolution of the Cold War, we begin by reminding ourselves how intricate is the society we are trying to analyze, and how much our speculative hypotheses are dependent upon selected fragmentary impressions and the culling of printed materials which refract more than they reflect even limited aspects of Soviet life. We direct our attention, therefore, not so much to broad general theories, nor to the propensities of the present Soviet individual leaders—about which we have little certain knowledge—but rather toward some of the underlying forces that seem to be at work, influencing the longer-term evolution of the Soviet system. From this perspective, our concern is not only with the conscious changes by the Soviet leadership, but even more so with those that may be partly or wholly unintended—the kind of transformations that come about over a period of time as the consequence of actions taken to meet immediate felt needs, but going far beyond the intentions and perhaps even the awareness of the actors themselves.

In response to a number of factors in international politics, as we saw in the previous chapter, the Soviet leadership has been brought to the view that greater emphasis upon the further development of its economy is  a fundamental key to the enlargement of its power and influence in the world. It is obvious that an arsenal of modern weapons systems and activities in outer space requires a highly developed technology supported by a strong economy. Further, the inhibitions against general war and the blunted promise of direct revolutionary action, in Europe at least, have combined to encourage reliance upon other instrumentalities for a long-term advance, including foreign aid, trade, and the example of a successful system, all of which add urgency to the repair of shortcomings in the domestic economy. Historically, the Soviet regime under Stalin had concentrated its resources upon rapid industrialization at all costs, with the result that spectacular advances in certain fields were purchased at the expense of others, chiefly agriculture and  consumer goods, as well as an increasingly inadequate system for administering the industrial complex that emerged. The effect of this unbalanced development could not be held off indefinitely. Declining growth rates and serious shortages in critical areas were but symptoms of profound, cumulative disorders which demanded attention. The Party was faced with the necessity of repairing the imbalances and adapting itself and its methods of governing to the requirements of administering an increasingly complex industrial society. Here we have, I believe, a fundamental factor in the transformation that has been taking place.

We are somewhat aware from our own experience how advancing industrialization continues to transform our own societies—shifting our populations, changing social patterns, complicating the functions of government and business organizations, creating an increasingly complex, delicate, and interdependent mechanism. How much more so is this the case for the Soviet Union, where the functions of control over all aspects of life are gathered in the hands of a small group of men. The contrast between the function of the Communist Party in the early days and now can be compared to the difference between running a Roman trireme, where coercion and exhortation were sufficient to keep the galley slaves pulling at their oars— and, on the other hand, operating a modern ocean vessel, where regularity of authority and highly developed leadership skills are required to encourage and coordinate the exercise of a variety of specialized functions. Responding to the requirements of industrialization, the Party leadership has been trying to find ways to modernize its system of administration and control, without—if possible—fundamental alterations in its political system.

Indeed, this last reservation is the question of questions for the Soviet system. Can so centralized a political control system efficiently administer an advanced industrial economy? If not, must it accept a metamorphosis in its fundamental political character? Can it do so, gradually, experimentally, without cataclysm?

These are the questions that loom over the process of deStalinization, which represented a major effort to chip away at the encrustations of bureaucratic inertia, of safe routines, cautious evasion of responsibility, and the paralysis of initiative, habits deeply imbedded in the middle generation of Soviet bureaucrats as part of the Stalinist heritage. Along with this have come other experimental efforts to modernize the system and make it more efficient: the reduction in the overt use of mass terror, to give a greater sense of personal security and to encourage initiative; more use of material incentives to raise productivity; an experimentation with market forces in place of over-centralized economic planning; somewhat wider latitudes in artistic and intellectual realms and in cultural and technical contacts with the West.

But, such is the nature of the Soviet system, these practical measures had to be given ideological rationalization and sanction, and this is the point at which friction bursts into flame between orthodoxy and the impulse to adapt and modernize. In the new Party program adopted in 1961, and elsewhere, the Party has sought to get away from its characterization as a dictatorship. In place of the previous self-description as a "dictatorship of the proletariat," it now seeks to identify the system as "a state of the whole people"—which is intended to carry the implication of a wider sense of voluntary participation by a classless population in the administration of the economy and the service functions of government. Along with this, the Party program identifies the present period as one in which the main task is "building Communism," which implies, but does not define, the promise of abundance widely shared.

Necessarily, these practical and ideological measures for the easement of internal tensions have been accompanied by a commitment to international peace as a positive motivation for popular support, in place of the earlier habit of mobilizing political support through the pressure of external tensions and hostilities. This has been registered on the ideological plane by the extended commitment to "peaceful coexistence" as a long-term strategy leading to ultimate victory, while the ups and downs of international tension have been accompanied by a broadened concept of struggle under conditions of "peaceful coexistence."

How far, then, does the model of totalitarianism still apply to the Soviet system under these conditions? A Soviet citizen, asked this question, would be likely to reply that the most important thing from his point of view is that the cruel and despotic use of mass terror has been mercifully eased. But from the point of view of an outside observer, the most significant characteristic of the regime is that control over all aspects of public life continues to be exercised by the governing group at the top of the Party, with the assistance of a still formidable police apparatus. Clearly, it would be misleading either to continue to apply the Stalinist model of totalitarian dictatorship, or to speak of liberalization in a Western sense. A more differentiated conceptual tool of analysis is required.

If a distinction is made between a traditional autocratic regime, which involves a high degree of concentration of political power and authority, and a totalitarian regime in which the control of all public aspects of life remains in the hands of one man or a small group and the society is not distinguished from the state, then what we know of the Soviet developments obliges us to regard the Soviet system as passing into some mature form of totalitarianism. We have learned a great deal in recent years about the structure and functioning of totalitarian systems, but we still know very little about the laws that govern their evolution under conditions of modern industrialization. Whether a mature form of totalitarianism can remain a more-or-less stable condition, or whether it is necessarily but a way-station on the path to pluralism and the diffusion of political controls, is of course the crucial and still unanswered question. Those writers who incline to the latter view tend to give much weight to the technocratic quality of the Party leadership, to the pressure of managers and functional interest groups, to the emergence of a "bourgeois middle class," and to the voices of protest of liberal intellectuals, artists, lawyers, or scientists.

It must be said, however, that so far at least these developments have not altered the essential structure of totalitarian control. There can be no doubt of the primacy of the small, coopting group at the top of the Party hierarchy exercising control through a large professional Party apparatus and a large political police apparatus, whose operations are more subtle and sophisticated than before, but no less pervasive into all aspects of life and especially those involved in contacts with foreigners. Even

casual and unsystematic investigation can identify significant groups in Soviet society with varying degrees of influence and a sense of group identity and group loyalty,
but the Party has so far succeeded in preventing such
groups from becoming political entities, with independent
sources of political power. This would include economic
administrators, managers, technocratic specialists, government bureaucrats, scientists, police, military, intellectuals,
artists, peasants, and the youth, as well as local and regional interest groups. These are of course very broad categories, and further significant distinctions can be made
within each of these groups. For example, conflicting
interest groups within the military establishment have
pressed their claims in public exchanges. Among the intellectuals there are some who function as spokesmen for
the Establishment and some bolder and more independent
spirits who press for modifications in Party control over
the arts, with the great majority somewhere ambiguously
in between.

We are, quite naturally, drawn to those among the
intellectuals and artists who voice aspirations for freer
expression, and who keep pressing, within the limits of
their situation, for less interference by Party functionaries
and for the expression of humane values in art. We are
right to recognize the universal moral significance of their
courage, but we are not right, and we do them a great
disservice, when we claim them as Westernized heroes.
For the most part, the liberal intellectuals as a group, including the younger generation of intellectuals, if one may
generalize from limited experience, appear to be patriotic
—in the sense that they are deeply committed to Russian

national traditions—and it must not be assumed that their pressure on the regime for less Party interference or their private criticism of particular officials is equated with a rejection of the system as a whole. Those few within this group who have an ideological commitment—and there are some, particularly among the young—idealize the Revolution in a pure sense, detached from the realities and the compromises that the Party has made. Most, however, are thoroughly and by deep habit apolitical: politics for them is the business of a disembodied, gray anonymous "they" who run things. As a group, they are not politically effective. Being an articulate segment of the population, and because of the functions they perform in the society, they do exert some pressure against one sector or another of the limits established by the governing group, but the prospects for their exercise of a dominant influence over the evolution of the system as a whole do not appear to be bright—the more so because "the system" in which they live is bulwarked by a large Party and police apparatus, which bureaucracy has a dynamic of its own.

It is particularly important, in considering the nature and influence of the liberal intellectuals, to be conscious of the difference between oral and printed levels of discourse in the Soviet Union. Even within official discussions, and even more so among the independent intellectuals, there is often a richness of thought and feeling of which only the most elliptical and hackneyed reflection is usually allowed by the Party functionaries to appear in journals, books, and newspapers. Printed materials are a constricted source of information and, therefore, our judgments on such matters must be based upon the testimony of sensitive observers and must be quite tentative.

The relationship of the ruling Party group to each of the functional groups and subgroups we have identified is a subtle process of interaction. Upward pressures do get registered and sometimes accommodated, the more so as the efficient functioning of the group is necessary to the system, but the accommodations are within well-defined limits of acceptance of the Party's ultimate control. This point is particularly important to appreciate in weighing the expectation that the technocrats are taking over the system. It is certainly true that the present Party leadership is better trained in technical and management experience than its predecessors have been;* it is also true that it is obliged to give weight to the imperatives reflected through the managers and the technical specialists. But the fundamental point is that the ultimate decision-making is still a political act, and it is securely in the hands of men whose vocation and experience are *primarily* those of political overseers, moving from one sector to another as needed.

We may be led into error if we analogize too directly from our own experience with "interest groups" and

---

*While writing the lines above, I fell to contemplating the plight of the obsolescent Party functionary, with the following half-serious result:

REVOLUTIONARY'S LAMENT

I, who survived the cavalry of the Czar,
Now find the Revolution becoming bizarre.
Our heirs are technicians with slide rule and glasses,
Above such things as the battle of classes.
The input was Marx and the output futility—
Our future is measured in marginal utility.

pressure lobbies, as some analysts tend to do. Undoubtedly functional interests have developed in the Soviet Union as part of the process of industrialization, and it seems to be the case that the process of decision-making increasingly provides for regularized consultation among the diverse interests affected, particularly in the post-Khrushchev period, but the Party's control of personnel in each of the other hierarchies and the shifting of Party personnel from one function to another tend to limit the independent pressure that any interest group can exert upon Party decision-making.

There is a question whether there is a Soviet equivalent to what in this country has come to be called "the military-industrial complex"—that is, some identification of groups that may have an interest in higher tension and in emphasizing the conflict aspect of foreign relations. It might appear from the available literature that certain of the military interests, certain of the heavy industrial interests, the Party professional ideologists, and the middle generation of the Party professional apparatus may be among the groups reflecting a commitment in this direction. But our group analysis is still largely an a priori affair, and we need to press our search for knowledge in this direction, in order that we may better identify the dominant political groups within the leadership and have some insight into their perceptions of the world, their values and their goals, as a differentiated matter, rather than generalizing about *the* Soviet leadership group as a whole. Group politics, within and outside the Party, obviously affect policy and personnel changes within the limits of a largely unified hierarchical system, but we cannot speak categorically about this, for the process is one of subtle personal interactions, permeated by informal private arrangements. It would, however, be stretching the evidence to suggest that the process yet resembles the interplay of independent pressure groups familiar to us.

Another misconception arises from the evident fact, immediately apparent to all travelers, that tastes have changed in the Soviet Union. From clothing styles to food, furniture, and architecture, the outer aspects of Soviet urban life have come to resemble those of urban life elsewhere, and many of the problems of urbanization, from the fragmentation of family life and the alienation of the individual to traffic congestion and city planning, have similar manifestations in Moscow and New York, London, or Paris. This has led some observers to conclude that a middle-class society is developing in the Soviet Union, whose conservative stamp will soon be felt upon Soviet political life. Of course, the appetites for consumer goods with quality and style as well as abundance constitute an undeniable political fact with which the Party leadership must reckon, but there is still a large political gap between this kind of pressure and the kind of middle-class political force that dominates West European or American politics today. Middle-class tastes do not a middle class make, at least not in the present context of the Soviet system, where the satisfaction of material aspirations is not correlated with wider participation in the political process.

It has been evident, even in this brief synthesis, that at each turn we are dealing with processes of change that

are subtle, ambiguous, and in motion. There is little em-
pirical evidence available, and it is extremely difficult to
say with certainty how far along the path any of these
processes have advanced or even to be sure in what direction they are moving. The main point that emerges, relevant to our concerns in these pages, is that it would be
premature to base present policy judgments upon an estimate that these domestic factors have already deflected
the main direction of Soviet foreign policy, although we
may want to encourage such possibilities over the long
run.

Certain more limited conclusions, however, do have a
bearing upon present policy formulation. It seems clearly
evident that domestic problems, particularly the repair
of economic deficiencies and the political consequences of
these reorganizations, occupy a position of high priority
in the attention of the Soviet leadership. It also appears
to be the case that the system has moved toward less reliance upon external tension for domestic consolidation
than formerly. Corresponding to the reduction in internal
tension, which is found useful in the operation of an
advancing industrial society, the leadership seems to find
the generation of external tension less useful in cementing
popular support and evoking productive energies than
the peace symbol, given the weary reaction of the population to the tragic effects of the last war, unless external
events appear to require a further mobilization of the
economy. It may also be the case that a broadening of the
decision-making process among a larger number of technical interests, also required by the complexity of the

economy, serves to impose some restraint upon the political leadership, reducing the possibility of sudden
changes, of dramatic surprise, and of caprice.

Beyond these limited and still tentative developments,
it is necessary to have a much longer time perspective in
mind in anticipating changes of a more profound character. Speculation about these possibilities is by no means
an idle endeavor, for it bears upon the question of how
our own actions may influence the course of these longer-
term developments. The present state of our knowledge,
however, does not support any monolinear theory. Among
the various theoretical models that have been advanced
in the West to describe the possible direction of Soviet
development—such as a further tightening of totalitarian
controls after the fashion of Orwell's *1984;* or a tradition-
alist direction, involving some form of pluralism and some
diffusion of power and authority; or an evolution in a
technocratic-bureaucratic direction—it is still largely
guesswork to say which of these, or whether some other
model, best fits the evidence we have.

Probably the determining factor is likely to center
around the future of the Party—whether the Party can
maintain its primacy and its essential character. The ideological authority of the Party has been weakened by the
deStalinization process, and by the present emphasis upon
economic progress rather than revolution. At the same
time, the structural authority of the Party has been
strengthened relative to other institutions. Whether the
erosion of ideological justification for the Party's command role will undermine its authority may depend primarily upon its success or failure in the management of

the economy. Perhaps it is something of a Marxist conception to argue that if the Party is successful in achieving a thriving economy this will produce its own kind of ideological justification, quite distant from its revolutionary origins. But if so, what would the ascendancy of technical specialists (and the passage of several generations) do to the values and goals of the Party? We are predisposed to hope that it will encourage liberal values, but might it not equally well tend toward an organization of society with greater efficiency, greater depersonalization, in which power is an end in itself, unrestrained by humane values? Some of these possibilities, of course, are but a magnification of those that concern us in examining the values of the Organization Man in our own society.

And can the economy be efficiently run? Can a system so highly centralized in its power structure adapt itself to the multiplicity of interdependent functions required by advanced industrialization? When one contemplates the present bureaucratic encumbrances that have barnacled Soviet planning, production, and distribution, the prospect does not seem favorable. Still, it would probably be a mistake to extrapolate from present economic troubles in the Soviet Union. We have had a tendency in the past to project too readily from Soviet successes at one time, or from its backwardness at another, and have been led into error as a consequence. Sometimes this is because both successes and backwardness are difficult to see in proportion, and also because it is difficult to estimate the flexibility of the Party leadership in dealing with the reallocation of resources.

Moreover, beyond the uncertainty whether the Party

will be able to repair present deficiencies and learn to administer so complex an economy, there is a further uncertainty whether the concentration of effort and resources provided by the Soviet system will turn out to have been upon the decisive levers of economic power. The criteria of success or failure may depend in part upon external factors. Whether a balanced development such as is now prized in the West, or a planned concentration upon certain sectors of the economy judged by the Soviet leaders to be decisive, will produce the more effective system may depend upon whether the world environment will favor peace and stability or continued mobilization, and, therefore, which forms of economic power will be the more influential.

In short, to return to our central question, while we may judge that the process of adaptation to advancing industrialization is a determining force, tending toward the ascendancy of technically trained executives and administrators, we cannot predict whether this will have the effect of diluting the Party's monopoly of power, or be internalized within the Party; nor can we be confident that it will tend toward a pluralism of independent forces within the society, from whose interplay will emerge a form of democracy defined and shaped by Russian historical and cultural experience. We may hope that this will be so, and we may, within the limits of our influence, try to encourage a development along these lines, but we should not assume that this is a determined outcome or that it has already begun to appear.

In any case, important as transformations in the Soviet system may prove to be in the longer run, they do not seem likely to be decisive in moderating the dynamism of Soviet foreign policy in the near future. The main factors that appear to shape Soviet foreign policy are those that grow out of the external environment. However much the Soviet leadership may wish in the present period to give priority to a domestic concentration of its energies, the outside world will not hold still. The flaring up of episodes to which the Soviet Union feels itself obliged to respond, the challenging competition of the Chinese regime, developments in Western policy, and other factors in international politics seem to be affecting domestic policy in the present period more than the other way around. It is to these external influences in the shaping of foreign policy that we now turn our attention.

# 4

# The Evolution of Soviet
# Foreign Policy and the
# Cold War

THE ABSENCE of a consensus in the West about how much or what kind of a threat is represented by Soviet or Chinese policy today, or by the international Communist movement, is probably the major reason for the divergence of policies among the Western allies. The spectrum of attitudes extends from those who see no reason for modifying their concern about Communism as a universal threat to domestic polity and world peace to those who are prepared to jettison the whole notion of a threat as having been a myth from the start, or as having become a myth as a result of changes in the Communist world. This is really the heart of the issue. This is where one must begin in judging the current relevance and effectiveness of Western policy with as much freshness of thought and precision of language as we can muster.

One of the persistent elements of confusion here has

been the role of Communist ideology in determining Communist behavior. It would be as much of an error, I believe, to dismiss the ideology altogether as it would be to take its pretensions literally. Nor is the truth to be found by splitting the difference, but rather by distinguishing between the various functions that ideology has performed in Soviet and other Communist behavior—particularly between the ideological vision of a world proletarian revolution, the Marxist–Leninist analytical approach to capitalism, and the Leninist guide to tactics, for each of these has been changing at a different rate, and each has had a different degree of operational significance. Moreover, it should be kept in mind that the validity of an ideological notion may be quite a separate question from its operational significance, since an idea, though wrong, may nevertheless be a political fact if people act upon it.

In the first chapter we sought to distinguish between prime causes and exacerbating factors in the early years of the Cold War, and we found ourselves brought to the conclusion that the ideological preconceptions of Communism must be assigned a prominent place among the prime causes. The whole notion of the Soviet revolution as a first episode in worldwide proletarian overturning of other governments, however unrelated to reality, predisposed the Soviet leaders to perceive hostility and inevitable conflict in its foreign relations, and provoked a fear abroad against the promise of "the worldwide triumph of Communist revolution"—a fear which reciprocally confirmed Soviet suspicions and nourished its expectations. During the long years of Soviet weakness this apocalyptic

vision bound to the Soviet Union a host of followers
abroad, whom it sought to use, more or less ineffectively,
as ancillary instruments of Soviet national interests—and
this too strengthened the picture of the Soviet Union as
the control center of an internationally coordinated con-
spiratorial movement dedicated to the unlimited goal of a
worldwide proletarian revolution against all other governments. We have already noted the fact that many other
sources of anxiety within Western societies contributed
to a disproportionate response in the West to the Soviet
challenge, resulting in a secondary exacerbation of the
conflict, and particularly focusing upon international
Communism as the indiscriminate source for a variety of
tensions.

As we have seen, the interacting hostility generated by
the Marxist conception of proletarian revolution, encouraged both by the Soviet Union and its adversaries, was
intensified in the years following the Second World War
by Soviet efforts to improve its national power position
in Eastern and Central Europe, flowing into territories
where traditional sources of resistance had been weakened
as a consequence of the war. Where that resistance was
supported, in the Eastern Mediterranean and in Western
Germany, the expansion of Soviet control stopped, leaving
a residual ambiguity whether the thrust had been moti-
vated primarily by national territorial aspirations or by a
renewal of international revolutionary ambitions. It seems
clearer in retrospect than it did at the time that the expansion into Eastern and Central Europe was, like most
of Soviet foreign policy, an action of the Soviet state in
pursuit of its national aspirations. The ideology of Com-

munism undoubtedly shaped the perceptions of the Soviet leadership in the way it came to believe that Soviet security required the total domination of the satellite states, but it has become increasingly clear that the goal of international proletarian revolution was essentially symbolic language for the advancement of Soviet national interests. Neither the reality of the Soviet state nor the principles that guided Soviet foreign policy have borne much correspondence to the symbolic ideological language of a Marxist proletarian international order, but the commitment to this vocabulary has persisted because the idealistic vision has had utility as a binding force between the Soviet regime and its adherents.

It is essential to distinguish, in our analysis, between the realities of Soviet behavior and the shadow play of verbal symbols if we are to clarify our understanding of the precise nature of the challenge to which we are seeking a response. In practice, Soviet foreign policy has been going through a very considerable evolution; as a consequence, the gap between its actual operating principles and the symbolic language of Marxist proletarianism has been widening.

When we speak of an "evolution" of Soviet policy, it is intended to distinguish this kind of change from short-term tactical shifts in policy, a distinction that is sometimes difficult to make in practice, for the significant long-term movements in Soviet foreign policy originate as temporary expedients which tend to become elongated in time, more elastic in application to cover occasional regressions, and finally more and more deeply embedded in doctrine. This has been the case with the strategy of "peaceful coexistence," which was drawn from earlier tactical responses to adverse situations requiring a breathing spell but has now been extended into a long-term strategy, implying a continuing acceptance of the necessity for an indirect and more political way of advancing Soviet interests than the militant advocacy of revolution and the use of force. To the Chinese, the Soviet leaders maintain that this is still a revolutionary policy, in the sense that it is the only effective and prudent way of proceeding, given the hazards of direct militant action in the world as it is today, and will ultimately lead to "the worldwide victory of Communism." This metamorphosis in the conception of revolution, becoming more indirect, more long-term, more dependent upon a variety of economic and political processes, is one way in which Soviet policy in practice seeks to maintain a tie with the sanction of the Marxist ideology, and, with it, a leading position in the international Communist movement.

The longer-term shifts in Soviet policy are best understood as the result of a process of adaptation, both conscious and unintended, chiefly in response to factors that shape the external environment. Among these, the most interesting (and most neglected) keys are to be found in the field of international politics—the political effects of modern weapons, of transportation and communications developments, of advancing industrialization, nationalism, decolonization, the rise of new nations, and the other changes discussed in Chapter 2. It is also important to be conscious of the fact that among other significant external factors influencing the course of Soviet policy has been the course of Western policy—the strategic military

power of the United States, the uses of that power in cir-
cumscribing Soviet freedom of action, and fluctuations
in Western firmness and cohesion in determining the external political environment. Also, of course, the intensification of the Sino-Soviet dispute and the process of
fragmentation of the Communist bloc must be listed both
as an effect of some Soviet policy changes and a cause of
further change. Finally, in this brief enumeration of the
principal causes of long-term change, must be listed the
domestic factors—the priority requirements of the Soviet
economy, internal political pressures, and the transformations in the Soviet system discussed in the previous chapter.
(This is not to denigrate the importance of domestic factors, including the role of leading personalities or fac-
tional disputes, in tactical situations, but it is intended to
give greater emphasis to the role of underlying forces in
the world environment in shaping the longer-term
evolution.)

To examine the effects of these factors in Soviet policy
in some further detail, it is illuminating to deal separately
with Soviet behavior toward the advanced industrial areas
and toward the underdeveloped areas, for an interesting
aspect of recent developments has been the differentiated
evolution of these two lines of policy.

In its policy toward the advanced industrial areas—
chiefly Western Europe and North America, and in certain respects, Japan—the Soviet Union appears to have
been influenced by two conflicting sets of considerations.

On the one hand, a certain stabilization has emerged
in relations with these areas, limiting the range of maneuver to fairly minor shifts of orientation in one country

or another. This relative stabilization has resulted from a combination of factors: the balance of mutual deterrence in the strategic weapons field; the firm resistance of Western policy to Soviet probes in this direction; and the economic growth of Western Europe, with political and social consequences unfavorable to revolutionary potentialities.

On the other hand, the advanced industrial areas are still of primary importance to the Soviet Union. Even though shifts within this area may be limited in their scope (as, for example, the effects of divisive issues within the Western alliance), such shifts can have decisive effects upon the relative power of the Soviet and the Western blocs. Industrial concentrations represent power in an immediate sense, although the orientation of the large populations of the underdeveloped world will be of considerable political importance over a more distant perspective. Moreover, the Soviet economic complex has no immediate need for the addition of raw materials or hungry and untrained populations from the underdeveloped world, but it can take advantage of industrial goods or grains from the West to ease points of strain in its economy, even temporarily.

The consequence of these conflicting considerations is that Soviet policy toward the advanced industrial areas has become increasingly a policy of political maneuver, whose primary concern is with power-bloc politics rather than the encouragement of revolutionary trends. The focus of its effort is to strengthen the Soviet bloc relative to the Western bloc, primarily by encouraging fragmenting trends in the West, and in particular the trend toward

a Europe independent of the United States. Whereas Soviet interest was formerly focused upon the proletariat
in the industrial countries, it now appears to accept the
fact that the working classes in these societies are neither
growing in size nor in revolutionary class-consciousness,
and Soviet interest has therefore shifted to the "bourgeoisie" as the politically effective lever through which it
hopes to influence the policy orientation of Western countries. To the "bourgeoisie," the Soviet appeal mutes all
talk of social revolution and seeks instead to address itself
to particular nationalist susceptibilities (for the purpose
of encouraging policies "independent" of the United
States), to opportunities for trade (both for reasons of
Soviet temporary economic requirements and also to develop interest groups in behalf of improved relations with
the Soviet Union), and to the theme of peace or détente.

One of the lessons of the Soviet experience over the
postwar period has been that Soviet interests are best
served by periods of reduced tension. Intra-Western differences flower when external tensions are eased, whereas
high East–West tension encourages Western cohesion and
military mobilization which reciprocally increases Soviet
military costs. Reduced tension is also the condition most
favorable to trade, the extension of credits, and access to
Western technological experience. The dominant trend
in Soviet policy, therefore, has been toward an atmosphere
of détente, although this has been subject to events and to
the operation of contradictory pressures upon the Soviet
leadership, which lead to great variations in the degree of
tension, still within the framework of what is formally
identified as a period of long-term "peaceful coexistence."

It is important however to distinguish between an atmosphere of détente and a rapprochement, because this has been a persistent source of confusion and disagreement in the West. To wish to operate in a climate of reduced tension does not necessarily imply a desire for political settlements, particularly on the key question of the future of Germany, which has not seemed subject to settlement unless one side or the other were willing to compromise its basic interests. In a certain paradoxical sense, the Soviet Union has become the advocate of the status quo in Europe, for one of its primary interests is to win acceptance from the West for Soviet interests in Eastern Europe and, in particular, Eastern Germany. What distinguishes this from real stabilization or what is sometimes anxiously, sometimes hopefully, called a "rapprochement" is that the basic political conflict persists, reflecting the fact that fundamental purposes are still far from harmonized. (Ideologically, this is expressed in the definition of "peaceful coexistence" as the most effective form of struggle, or competition.) The political conflict, though restrained by the climate of détente, expresses itself through continued manipulation of divisive issues—encouragement of the "national independence" of General de Gaulle, an alternate play upon the Greeks and the Turks to heighten their tensions over the Cyprus issue, or, in its broadest dimension, efforts to encourage the emergence of the "New Europe" as a power grouping detached from the United States.

In practice, the policy of détente has been subject to considerable degrees of inflection. Of late there has been less calculated alternation between periods of tension and periods of relaxation as a deliberate tactic, since the application of tension generally produced results disadvantageous to the Soviet Union, but even so the level of tension is subject to developments elsewhere and cannot always be controlled or compartmentalized. During certain periods, the climate of détente has extended to the United States, as during 1959 and 1963; at other times, there have been differentiated degrees of tension in the policies addressed to the United States and to the various countries of Western Europe. During periods in which the atmosphere of tension between the Soviet Union and the United States has been reduced, problems both domestic and diplomatic have bedeviled the Western alliance, and we shall want to consider in our next chapter whether it is possible to hold the alliance together under conditions of reduced tension.

The reduction of tension has also encouraged tendencies toward fragmentation within the Communist movement, and one consequence of this process that is likely to be of increasing importance to political developments in Western Europe is the change that has been emerging in the character and the role of the West European Communist parties. The most eloquent articulation and rationalization of this trend is to be found in the memorandum written by the Italian Communist leader, Palmiro Togliatti, shortly before his death in the autumn of 1964. This document is of profound importance in defining the pressures upon the Western European Communist parties to adapt their operations to the social conditions now prevailing, rather than to the Bolshevik-Marxist stereotype of a rising revolutionary proletariat.

Adherence to the Marxist orthodoxy has resulted in sterility and isolation, Togliatti argued, and it is necessary for the Communist parties of the West to face present-day political and social realities. Accordingly, the Communist parties of the West have been seeking to function within their respective national systems, to become the authentic voice of radical protest, as in some measure they have done in France and Italy, although they have been limited in these efforts by the incubus of their attachment to Moscow and by their authoritarian forms of organization. In the case of the Italian Communist Party, subservience to Moscow has been considerably weakened, and open debate within the Party has suggested that some democratization of its procedures may be possible. If so, and if other European Communist parties follow the Italian lead, a new and important factor in European politics may emerge, which could substantially shift to the left the center of gravity of the coalitions which have more or less dominated European political life. Whether under these conditions the West European Communist parties could become genuinely independent, returning to their pre-Comintern Social Democratic and anarcho-syndicalist traditions, or whether, as seems more likely, they will retain an ambiguous tie to Moscow as quasi-appendages of a loosely articulated Communist movement, will be a decisive question.

Even now, however, there has already emerged a semi-autonomous West European grouping of Communist parties, seeking to identify itself with European radical left traditions, and to attract European intellectuals groping for a present-day radicalism which defines itself in novel, post-Marxist terms. Many writers of the left in Europe, in and out of the Communist movement, have been probing the question of the proper function of radicalism in societies where relative abundance has attenuated the class struggle, and where, as a consequence, Western socialism has been moving increasingly in a reformist direction. The attention of some has centered upon questions concerning the quality of life under conditions of industrialism, and it may be on this terrain that Western democracy will have to meet its new challenge. It seems improbable, however, that a radicalism so oriented would ever accept the discipline from the East that eviscerated its predecessors or would accept the leadership of Party officials who served as organizational appendages to the Soviet apparatus in the name of proletarian internationalism.

For its part, the Soviet Union has been jockeying for some kind of leadership over the Western Communist parties despite the organizational complications of the Sino-Soviet dispute, which greatly increased the opportunities of the national parties for maneuver. It is clear, however, that the paramount consideration from the Soviet point of view is the weight of these parties in international Communist politics, rather than potential service within their respective countries. Least of all does the Soviet Union regard itself as dependent upon the Western Communist parties as instruments of revolution. If anything, they are regarded as ancillaries of limited usefulness to Soviet diplomacy: mildly useful for mounting demonstrations that can be represented as a reflection of popular attitudes; potentially useful for clandestine activity in the event of war, but relatively ineffective as political make-weights.

Meanwhile, the language of proletarian international-ism continues to be the lingua franca of the movement, although it becomes increasingly archaic. If the goal of world revolution is operationally irrelevant, however, the Marxist–Leninist analysis of Western societies with some modifications retains an important function in shaping the perceptions and expectations underlying Soviet diplo-macy—for example, the Soviet expectations that the "bourgeoisie" as a class can be induced for reasons of short-term private profit to act contrary to its long-term political interests, or that "contradictions" are inherent in domestic and intra-West relations. High growth rates in the West have shaken but have not dispelled Soviet antici-pations for the future, which still rely upon stereotyped conceptions of the rigidities in Western social structures.

The fact that neither the Soviet Union nor the Western Communist parties have any expectation of communizing the countries of Western Europe in the foreseeable future does not mean that Soviet policy toward this area can be dismissed as irrelevant or unimportant. However, it must be understood primarily as a striving for political advan-tage in the power-bloc competition over a fairly long perspective. It has always in mind such questions as: what will Europe look like five or ten years from now? It is deeply preoccupied with its analysis of the emerging po-litical and social forces within the Western industrial countries, and with such semi-ideological questions as the role of cartels in the integration process; and, on the ex-ternal side, with the essential question whether the continent will be within or outside the American sphere of influence and, in the latter case, whether it will be dominated by the Federal Republic of Germany. Indeed, the question of the future power of the Federal Republic is one of obsessive centrality in Soviet diplomacy toward Europe.

For the present, Soviet diplomacy toward the West is a holding action. It operates under restraints that reflect a preoccupation with serious domestic problems and an awareness of the limitations of the present Soviet strategic position. It appears to desire nothing more than to have the West hold quiet for a while, so that it will not be distracted from the priority tasks of repairing structural deficiencies in the Soviet economy and divisions within the Communist bloc. In the recent past (that is, since October 1962) it has pressed neither for major competitive gains nor for major settlements. We are, so to speak, on the back burner.

In a sense, it has been a cold détente, for the possibilities of substantive settlements have been diminished by the conflict in Southeast Asia and by the unrelenting Chinese criticism of the Soviet leadership as insufficiently militant. Any dealings with "the imperialists" are exploited by the Chinese as "capitulationism," and the Soviet leadership smarts under, and is effectively inhibited by, the charge. The Soviet Union seems to feel that its own interests require a détente of some sort with the West, but for the present, while the conflict in Vietnam is acute, and until its leaders decide that the Soviet Union would gain more support within the Communist world as champions of peace than as militants they remain unable to move toward any substantive improvement of relations with the West.

Conversely, if militancy produces gains for China, the pressures upon the Soviet leadership will be strengthened to move in that direction, either in concert or in competition with the Chinese.

Therefore, the future of "peaceful coexistence" as a long-term strategy toward the industrial areas of the West is now subject to the interplay between these two factors —the Sino-Soviet dispute and the involvement of the great powers in local conflicts in the underdeveloped areas.

Over the past decade, Soviet policy toward the underdeveloped areas has also been evolving toward a longer-term and more indirect political strategy and has been requiring an increasing share of Soviet attention and resources. The development has taken place in a series of stages and has been deeply affected by the complications of the Sino-Soviet dispute.

Beginning about 1954 and 1955, the possibilities for steering the onrushing colonial independence movement and gaining some advantage from the various shades of neutralism and nonalignment began to attract the Soviet leadership to a more sustained effort in this direction. From the earliest days of the Revolution, the colonial independence movement had been an integral part of the Communist world picture, but had received only sporadic support until the surge of nationalism in Asia and Africa, in contrast to the increasing stabilization in Europe, seemed to point to this area as the most promising theater of action. Moreover, jet aircraft and radio communication extended the reach of operations to such a degree that physical containment was quickly rendered obsolete.

The essential purpose of Soviet efforts in this period was not to strive for immediate control over these areas, but in the first instance to deny them to the West, by drawing nationalist leaders of the underdeveloped world into a loose coalition of anti-Western states. The trend of Soviet policy was therefore identified as "working with the national bourgeoisie," and it was more concerned with influencing the orientation of these nationalist leaders in world politics than in overthrowing them by revolutionary action on the part of the local Communist parties, which formally remained on the Communist agenda, subject to continuous postponement in the face of receding prospects for successful revolutionary action. It should be noted that a policy of this kind added to the reliance upon Soviet economic development as a key lever of foreign policy, since the economy's attractiveness as a model of development was intended to constitute a major appeal to nationalist leaders seeking relevant experience on the path to rapid industrialization. Moreover, the goods needed for selective foreign aid were for the most part the kinds of things that were in short supply at home.

On the whole, the optimism with which the Soviets entered into active operations in the underdeveloped areas was not long sustained. The nationalist leaders proved to be more independent in fact than was expected; nonalignment began to take on its own mystique and would not remain dependably pliant to Soviet guidance; moreover, the nationalist leaders insisted upon indigenous forms of economic and social development and did not define "socialism" in the same way that the Soviet Union did, nor were they wholly responsive to Soviet leadership in the United Nations or in international politics. The Soviet experience in the Congo was a particularly trying one, disappointing Soviet hopes that the United Nations would perform what it euphemistically called "an objectively progressive role" in preparing the way for Soviet-supported factions to gain control. Soviet policy was also limited by having at its disposal relatively few technicians who were intimately familiar with the language and culture of the underdeveloped areas, and the Soviet Union began to realize that less spectacular but more substantial long-term gains would require careful preparation of cadres and a supporting body of research institutes. Moreover, economic difficulties raised questions whether the drain of foreign assistance programs was worth a higher priority than competing claims for resources at home. The one success of this period—Cuba—came about through the unforeseen conversion of a nationalist middle-class–led revolution; Soviet efforts to generalize the experience as a new form of "national democracy" have not proved applicable elsewhere, with the possible exception of Indonesia where the benefit of such a conversion might in the future redound to China.

As the dispute with China began to erupt into open polemics, Soviet policy toward the underdeveloped regions came under fire as a central issue. China not only attacked the Soviet policy as one that neglected revolutionary opportunities, but also moved to exploit these opportunities by aggressive competition against the Soviet Union for leadership in Asia, Africa, and Latin America.

Declaring that the main theater of revolutionary action was indeed in the underdeveloped world, China began to develop a Maoist variant of Leninism which addressed itself to all possible sources of discontent and protest, including nationalism, color, race, poverty, imperialism, and local landlords, and charged its appeal with an intense revolutionary militancy. To the Soviet surprise, the economic limitations under which the Chinese operated have not prevented them from making remarkable progress, largely because of the great appeal of the dynamism of Chinese militancy in these areas, in contrast with the more measured political line of Soviet policy, conscious of its interests elsewhere. China has signaled its intention of forming a new international, claiming the true banner of Marxism–Leninism, but so far at least the reach of its power to disrupt is greater than its power to control, and it seems to feel that it has more leverage as a dissident member of the present Communist group of nations and parties than it would have as the leader of its own.

At the same time, in the broader field of international politics outside the Communist movement, China has skillfully used diplomatic techniques as well, where circumstances require relations with existing governments. It has systematically sought to isolate India by arrangements with its neighbors; it has tentatively explored the possibility of an "intermediate zone," linking France, Japan, and the neutral countries in a loose alliance directed equally against the Soviet Union and the United States; it has given tentative encouragement to Sukarno's effort to organize NEFOS (the New Emerging Forces) as a possible counter to the United Nations; and, more importantly, it has sought to develop a Bandung bloc of the Afro-Asian nations under its leadership, claiming proprietary rights to the slogan of "anti-imperialism," trying to keep the Soviet Union elbowed aside from interfering in what it regards as its own political domain. Peking is crowded these days with the sales representatives of Western companies or combines, and their desire for private profit is exuberantly manipulated for diplomatic advantage by Chinese purchasing officials.

While it is still too early to judge the success of these Chinese efforts, it is already clear that they have resulted in a shifting trend in Soviet policies toward the underdeveloped areas. Responding to the necessities of a two-front conflict, against the Chinese on the one side and the West on the other, and to the variety of conditions that have divided the "third world" so deeply that it cannot any longer be considered as a unit in world politics, the Soviet Union has been moving toward further differentiations in both theory and practice.

In those situations where the existing governments have been more or less stabilized, Soviet policy has tended to strengthen its relations with the "national bourgeoisie" —warmly in the case of those who lean the right way in their nonalignment, less so where the Western influence remains strong (situations defined by the Soviet Union as "neocolonial"). No longer does the Soviet Union inveigh against "Arab socialism," or other indigenous varieties of social organization, as it formerly did. Local Communist parties have been submerged within local nationalist movements, and exert their influence through non-Communist organizations and publications. (This policy has shown some fluctuation, in response to an intense internal debate over the degree of separate identity that should be maintained by the local Communist parties.) Selectively, the Soviet Union relies upon its capacity for economic assistance to give practical weight to its diplomacy in competition with the Chinese. While so far at least Soviet diplomacy has not been notably successful in its relations with these "stabilized" states of the underdeveloped world, its perspective seems to be a longer-term one than it was in the first flush of its optimism a decade ago, and it now counts upon the cultivation of the next generation of political leaders in these areas and the better preparation of its own specialists.

However, in those areas where active conflict exists, as a result of tribal, ethnic, or power-group rivalries, or in those few instances of persisting colonial relationships, the Soviet Union has given more militant meaning to its ambiguous doctrine of support for "wars of national liber-ation," which sanctions Soviet military, political, or eco-nomic assistance for any local conflict situation which the Soviet Union chooses to define as a national liberation struggle. (And where, by definition, Western aid for the opposition automatically becomes "aggression in support of counter-revolution.") In such local conflict situations, the present greater Soviet militancy is an effort to main-tain its leadership in the Communist movement by refut-ing the Chinese charge of lack of enthusiasm for local revolutionary developments. Even more broadly, it is a response to the competition of the Chinese for leadership of the nationalist movements in the underdeveloped areas under the banner of "anti-imperialism." Where the Chinese are active, or potentially active, the Soviet Union finds restraint difficult, particularly because the provocation of "imperialist" involvement is regarded as advantageous from the point of view of Chinese strategy, for it impales the Soviet Union most painfully upon the dilemma of its multiple interests.

In short, the combination of continued turbulence in the underdeveloped areas and the emergence of a Maoist radical revolutionary drive works against the prospects for a conservative Soviet policy in these areas, and has a secondary disturbing effect upon the prospects for stabilization elsewhere, since it leads the Soviet Union to give a militant inflection to its policies with regard to the campaign for "anti-imperialism" and support for "wars of national liberation." The probabilities appear to be that these factors of disturbance will grow rather than diminish, and may increasingly dominate the international scene. The conditions required to mitigate this trend would have to include a change in Chinese policy as a result of its demonstrated lack of success and/or a Soviet decision to give higher priority to a global policy of "peaceful coexistence." In the latter case, it is conceivable that the Soviet leadership would find its self-interest served by the development of international mechanisms to contain and pacify the many local conflicts that seem likely to continue to roil the underdeveloped world. Despite conflicting expectations regarding future political trends in these areas, the West and the Soviet Union may find at least a minimum overlap of self-interest in preventing or containing the outbreak of violence whose widening effects cannot be foretold.

It has become a commonplace by now to observe that the Communist bloc is no longer monolithic, and perhaps should no longer even be called a bloc. This is not the place for a full review of the Sino-Soviet dispute, or of the process of fragmentation in Eastern Europe and among the Communist parties, but some observations are required on the effects of these transformations upon the Cold War.

It seems clear that what we are now dealing with is not Communism, but many communisms. The word has come to have quite different operational significance in the various parts of the world and requires a wide range of responses rather than an indiscriminate fear and hostility. The problem has a different and more complicated form than it was thought to have in the early years of the Cold War, but it has not, as some suggest, eliminated itself. The separate elements of the Communist movement still have vitality and international significance, and there are practical limits on how far the centrifugal forces within the bloc can operate, even in the extreme case of the Sino-Soviet dispute.

The most evident effect of the fragmentation is that Soviet power is weakened, distracted, and circumscribed by these developments. The euphoric optimism which saw the accession of Eastern Europe and China to the Communist bloc as confirmation of the unstoppable flow of history toward Communist ascendancy has been replaced by a mood of weary self-examination, coping with complexity and disrepair everywhere at once. The Soviet leadership finds itself at the same moment struggling to discover by experimentation the principles of a more resilient control system that can replace the ruthless coercion of Stalinism, both at home and in Eastern Europe, while with the other hand it is obliged to carry on a hapless duel with an aggressive and uncompromising Chinese challenger. To say that the effect is distracting is an understatement, but the way in which this influences Soviet policy is somewhat different in Eastern Europe than in Asia.

In its relations with the Communist states of Eastern Europe, including Yugoslavia, the Soviet Union has found the invocation of the slogan of "proletarian internationalism" increasingly ineffective in stemming the resurgence of nationalism. "Proletarian internationalism" has meant an acceptance of the primacy of the interests of the Soviet Union as the homeland of Revolution, but as the reality of the Revolutionary grail faded, with it disappeared the claims of Soviet national interest as an overriding organizing principle for the Communist group of nations and parties. The underlying forces that contributed to this increase of nationalism included the process of industrialization within the Soviet Union, which by stimulating the deStalinization campaign was to signal the dissolution of the rigid Stalin control system in Eastern Europe; the economic growth of both Eastern and Western Europe, and the consequent interest in increased political and economic relationships between the two; the relaxation of international tension; the pressures upon the Soviet system and the Communist regimes in Eastern Europe to justify themselves primarily in terms of their economic performance; and the Soviet need to bid for the support of the separate Communist parties in the organizational in-fighting of the Sino-Soviet dispute.

The effect of these pressures was to move the Soviet bloc in Europe toward a conception of its relations modeled in theory somewhat after the British Commonwealth, and in practice after a traditional hegemonical alliance, frankly accepting a certain flexibility in degrees of allegiance on the basis of separate national interests. The broad limits within which this diplomatic flexibility operates are set on one side by formal adherence to the Warsaw Pact and the reliance of the Party elite in each country upon the ultimate sanction of Soviet power; on the other by the reliance of the Party elites upon nationalism and the drive for economic improvement as domestic sources for popular acceptance. Within these broad limits, the regimes of Eastern Europe have fluctuated both in their degree of independence from Soviet control and in their easement of totalitarian controls in their own societies—these two currents of change not always operating congruently with one another. One other point that is worth adding here is that the Eastern European Communist states, including Yugoslavia, have had a marked effect in encouraging experimentation with measures of economic rationalization within the Soviet Union, and together with the Communist Party of Italy have also encouraged the widening of Soviet latitudes in cultural controls. To some extent it can be said that these parties have an osmotic function in transmitting Western influences into the Soviet system.

We have earlier referred to the trend toward semi-autonomous regional groupings of Communist parties, especially in Western Europe, where some competition for regional leadership has developed between the Italian and the French parties, the latter acting in behalf of the

Soviet Union. On the issue of the Communist assessment of, and strategy toward, the European Common Market, the Italian Communist Party has made leading contributions, partly because of the pressures it feels to hold a broadly based labor movement intact and to broaden its appeal to the Italian Socialists. Again, the Italian party, together with the Yugoslav and Romanian parties, has exercised a restraint on the desire of the Soviet leadership to move to a decisive showdown conference with the Chinese, and they have, through their own initiatives, defined in practice the characteristics of "national Communism" and a theory of loose bloc collaboration under the slogan, "unity in diversity."

But if it is the case that the limited autonomy which has developed in the Communist movement in Eastern and Western Europe has contributed to the conscious acceptance of the decline in force of such basic ideological conceptions as "proletarian internationalism," "monolithic unity," and "proletarian world revolution," and has encouraged instead a frank recognition of traditional nation-state interests, the same cannot be said for the effect of the fragmentation of the Communist movement elsewhere. As we have seen, the effect of the challenge of Chinese revolutionary orthodoxy on the plane of ideology and revolutionary competition on the plane of action has been to check equivocal trends in the Soviet Union toward moderation in its policies toward the underdeveloped areas.

Although the Sino-Soviet polemic exchanges obliged the Soviet Union to go much further in articulating the premises of its strategy of "peaceful coexistence" than it had heretofore done, the challenge from the left, to which the Soviet leadership has always reacted defensively, inhibited the Soviet Union from developing a theoretical rationale for the adaptations in policy which had emerged under the name of "creative Marxism." Instead, it was obliged to renounce "revisionism," and to deny that its policies represented any fundamental theoretical departures.

On the plane of action, the Soviet leadership was vulnerable to a challenge against its policies in the underdeveloped areas because it had suffered from equivocation and internal disagreement in developing its policies toward the former colonial areas and the local conflicts in these areas. While Soviet theorists had gone quite far in recognizing that a general nuclear war, however it began, would result in no absolute gain and perhaps little relative advantage, they had not been of the same unanimity with regard to the hazards of local conflicts. Some authorities argued that the risk of escalation through the involvement of the nuclear powers made such local conflicts dangerous, and they therefore urged by implication a conservative policy in this direction. Others argued that the mutual inhibitions against the use of nuclear weapons now reduced the risk of giving conventional support to parties involved in local conflicts defined as "wars of national liberation." Those who shared this view saw the continuation of an active revolutionary front in the underdeveloped areas, and urged that "anti-imperialism" and "anti-colonialism" be made the keynotes of Soviet policy, at the expense if necessary of the themes of "peaceful coexistence" and "disarmament."

The effect of the Sino-Soviet dispute has been to strengthen the latter approach, for as a practical matter the Soviet leadership found that the Western front did not hold either much promise of substantive negotiations on the one hand or much danger of Western initiative on the other, and could be held relatively quiet with a non-substantive atmosphere of relative détente; the under-developed area was, however, inherently unstable, and presented the immediate question whether the leadership of the nationalist, anti-imperialist dynamic would be grasped by the Maoist movement, still fervently com-mitted to a world revolutionary outlook.

To return now to the question with which the chapter began: what should be the focus of our concern? How have these diverse trends in the evolution of Soviet foreign policy affected the nature of the Cold War?

Amid many elements shrouded in ambiguity, the one point that stands out clearly is a negative one: that the spectre of international Communist revolution is a myth. It belongs in the world of verbal symbols and not in the world of actual behavior. Neither the Soviet claims to the symbols of "socialism," "homeland of the working-class," "proletarian internationalism," and so on, nor the night-mare of Western conservatives in which the workers of the world unite under the Soviet banner, deserve to be taken seriously. This is not to say that we have nothing to worry about. We do, but this stereotype which has served as the focus for so many anxieties is not one of them, and it should not continue to cloud our perception of the present actual situation.

We have observed that the transitional development in Soviet foreign policy over the past decade or more has been increasingly toward traditional nation-state diplomacy. This is particularly true in Soviet policy toward the advanced industrial countries, and to a lesser degree toward the relatively stabilized states of the underdeveloped area; it is even true in some degree toward the former satellite states of Eastern Europe. We are approaching the fiftieth anniversary of the Soviet Revolution, and it is possible to say that very little of the Marxist apocalyptic goal of world proletarian revolution has survived this half century other than as ritualistic language. The slogan of "ultimate worldwide triumph of Communism" continues to have a hortatory function, but it expresses a reliance upon the forces of history rather than a rallying cry for revolutionary activity, and even as such it recedes into the indefinite future. That part of the ideology which serves an analytical function—the analysis of capitalism, or convictions about the inevitable course of future history, has also been subject to modification, although much less so. This part of the ideology does continue to have an operational meaning, affecting the way in which the Soviet leadership perceives the world and interprets its national interest, although generational changes within the leadership are apparent in the degree to which actual data from the outside world and direct observation are accepted as modifying and sophisticating ideological preconceptions.

The main point here is that the deepening commitment over the past decade to "peaceful coexistence" as a strategy reflects a significant evolutionary response to external necessity, and an attenuation of even a verbal commitment to the goal of a worldwide revolution. (It should no longer be necessary to point out, each time the term is used, that "peaceful coexistence" is to be understood as an active, though not unrestrained, policy of pursuing national advantages by indirect and long-term means.)

The question has naturally arisen whether this trend is so deeply established that it cannot be reversed. Might it not be possible, some writers have asked, for another strong figure to emerge who would take hold of the machinery of government as Stalin did and direct it toward a policy of uncompromising militancy? Or, might a "Chinese" faction become ascendant within the Soviet leadership, and argue that the "peaceful coexistence" line had proved unproductive and should be replaced by greater militancy not only in the underdeveloped areas, but generally? Particularly, the argument goes on, might this not be the case if China is allowed to reap gains from its militancy, if the West is weak and divided, if local opportunities present themselves where militant action might seem to be advantageous?

Certainly no one can say categorically that such a turn is impossible, although there are many factors that make it seem improbable. Domestically, the requirements of industrialization and the aroused expectations of the population for improved living conditions would make a reversion to tighter controls and higher mobilization extremely difficult in the absence of a threatening crisis. Externally, all the factors we have enumerated as requiring the extension of "peaceful coexistence"—the continued rise of productivity in the West and the consequent decline in class tensions, the relative inutility of the foreign Communist parties, the increasing dependence upon the Soviet economy as a principal lever of foreign policy as well as the major justification for the dominant role of the Party, the strategic power of the West, its firm responses to expansionist probes, and the adverse effects of such probes—all the factors that made Stalinism seem dysfunctional, would argue against such a reversion. As long as these conditions continued to be part of the "objective situation," only a tide of irrationality, or the workings of a powerful domestic political upheaval, would seem likely to reverse the present evolutionary trend. We are still too close to the events that led to the Second World War to dismiss the possibilities of an irrational tide in any society, but we should also be conscious of the fact that many of the barriers to such behavior depend upon what we do, a point to be discussed further in the next chapter.

Of course, this does not exclude the possibility of inflections of the policy of "peaceful coexistence" toward somewhat greater militancy from time to time (which some writers loosely describe as a "turn toward world revolution") or particularly a heightened effort to capture the nationalist revolutionary movements for its own purposes, but the difference of degree between this and a total abandonment of the underlying trend should not be obscured.

What follows from this? If we have correctly characterized the present direction of Soviet policy, what then is the actual nature of the challenge to which we should be directing our responses? If it is not the menace of Marxist revolution, what is the problem?

First of all, we should not lose sight of the fact that the greatest threat to our security at the present time is the formidable military power of the Soviet Union in its confrontation with Western strategic military power. This is the number one problem despite the fact that the probabilities of a deliberate Soviet military attack seem low, and hazards other than military are more likely to be realized, but the potential destructiveness of these weapons is so catastrophic that even a low probability of their use remains a dominant concern. This includes not only Soviet intercontinental missiles, whatever their number may be, but also the missiles of lesser range targeted on West Europe, and the still formidable Soviet conventional forces available to the European theater, which remains a potential locus of conflict particularly because of the unresolved problem of a divided Germany, apparently unresolvable in the near future.

Within recent years we have grown complacent about this danger because of the present strategic stabilization and the growing sobriety on all sides about the risks of general nuclear war, but the stabilization is tenuous and does not constitute a sufficient guarantee against unimaginable destruction. Advances in military technology, miscalculation, or the action of third parties could sweep aside the present apparent stability—the more so because military power is engaged, in some indefinable degree, in the background of every encounter where political advantages are at stake. This demands to be listed first among

the threats to our security, no less so because it is also the
major threat to Soviet security, and that of everyone else.

Second, there is the plane of political rivalry on which
the Soviet Union strives to increase its power, influence,
prestige, and security as a nation-state against the existing
distribution of power in the world. Although less immediately hazardous to the world than a direct frontal
challenge by force, and although subject to tacit restraints
that have grown up in practice in recent years, this expression of fundamentally opposed objectives is deadly
serious, and could if unopposed lead to Soviet dominance
in international politics. This is the "struggle" side of the
strategy of "peaceful coexistence," and it is reflected in
multitudinous daily activities of Soviet diplomacy, ranging from interference with barge traffic to West Berlin
to large-scale marketing of crude oil to Italy, calculated
shifts of political support as between France and the
Federal Republic, exploitation of disarmament negotiations for political advantage, procedural incapacitation
of the United Nations, use of selective technical assistance
and economic aid to gain political advantages, cultural
exchanges aimed at propaganda or technological borrow-
ing, and so on. In the shadows of this overt diplomatic
activity, espionage and subversion are the province of
special bureaucracies whose outlook is closer to military
hostility than to diplomatic rivalry.

How should this plane of conflict be assessed? In some
of its aspects, it represents the "normal" competitive striving of all nation-states in the jungle of international politics. Other nations, including our own, are not free from
many of the same practices, although the difference in de-

gree reflects the extent to which Soviet purposes are opposed to a conception of a stable international order, more
or less building on the present system of nation-state relations. The question of degree here is vital, for beneath the
ambiguities of national rivalries there is a certain flux in
the dividing line between competitive conflict and the
acceptance of the on-going system. The response required
is therefore a dual one: to recognize as deadly earnest this
plane of conflict and compete with it effectively, and at
the same time to draw the Soviet Union further toward a
recognition of its own long-term self-interest in subordi-
nating its striving for competitive advantage to an enlarged sphere of international cooperation. The Soviet
Union is not the only problem here: the subordination of
sovereign nationalisms to a framework of international
cooperation, however rudimentary at this stage, would be
difficult enough in itself, but the problem is made more
complicated by the suspicious negativism with which the
Soviet Union habitually regards all international mechanisms not subject to its control.

Third, there is the multiple challenge of Chinese Communism. Twenty years of revolutionary effort against
great odds have left the Chinese Communist leadership
with a heady sense of riding an unstoppable wave, a deep
commitment to revolutionary techniques and goals, and
an intense emotional hostility against "Western imperialism." Fifteen difficult years of nation-building have not
diminished the Chinese determination to reassert traditional Chinese interests in Asia, and in particular to gain
control of Taiwan, sooner or later, by one means or another. The Chinese ambition to play the role of a great

power, despite mountainous difficulties in developing its economy, is reflected in worldwide diplomatic activity, seeking to assert leadership over an "anti-imperialist" coalition of Afro-Asian states. The passionate commitment of the present generation of Chinese Communist leaders to revolutionary objectives is demonstrated in the activation of a Maoist radical revolutionary movement that serves as a catalyst of violence throughout Asia, Africa, and Latin America, stimulating racial conflict, and, as we have observed, exerting a militant pressure against Soviet evolutionary trends toward restraint. More alarming still is the prospect that the Chinese Communist leadership may one day have at its disposal a stockpile of nuclear weapons and a missile delivery system, before time and events may have lent moderation and responsibility to its policies. In the meantime, Chinese recalcitrance is a major complicating factor in the effort to introduce international safeguards into the arms confrontation. The West has not begun, in any concerted way, to face the broad questions raised by the multiple facets of the Chinese challenge, to consider how to mitigate present dangers while exerting its influence toward rendering the longer-term relationship less hazardous.

Fourth, there is the sector of the problem that arises out of local Communist action in the underdeveloped areas. Here indeed the purely Communist problem begins to lose itself in the larger current, for Communism here tends to be a complication rather than a prime cause. The sources of upheaval in the underdeveloped world are not Communist in inspiration and will not respond to a policy of anti-Communism.

A blanket analysis will not serve for these areas, for it tends to obscure the distinctions that are the essence of the problem. It is difficult in the first place to distinguish the Communist component of the problem from the force of nationalism and the political expression of economic and social protest. Within the Communist groups, it is often not easy to discern the lines of control to Moscow or to Peking, or to assess the degree of local autonomy. The term "Communist" may mean anything from a disciplined adherent to Soviet or Chinese control to a rebel who has no other name to give his rebellion.

In the triangular competition between the Soviet Union, China, and the West to guide the erupting forces of these areas, the West has the disadvantage of being associated with the hated symbol of imperialism and of representing a social system and a culture that seem irrelevant to local needs. On the other hand, the West has the advantage of representing great material progress, which exercises a powerful attraction even in its frivolous manifestations. The West can also have the advantage of disinterestedness, for its interests are best served by assisting local societies to maintain their independence and to move toward improved living conditions in a nonviolent way. To do this, however, it is not enough to hold off the incursions of Chinese or Soviet agents under the banner of anti-Communism. The Western program must have a positive political content which is relevant and attractive, and, preferably, the West should have the political acuity to act before violence has erupted and before the potentially constructive elements of the local society are squeezed out between the political extremes.

This is an unaccustomed task, for the political organization of a transitional society is very different from the Western experience, and we have for a long while assumed that our own line of development had a universal validity, inattentive to the values of other cultures and traditional societies than our own or to the dilemma of democracy in local situations where modernization seems to require a concentration of authority. We alienate our potential allies, and through ignorance range ourselves against the forces of change. The slowness of the West to become sensitive to local political realities has been due in large measure to the fact that the West, and the United States in particular, has approached the problems of the underdeveloped areas primarily as a sector of the fight against Communism.

The frenetic and simplistic preoccupation with the Cold War, which tended to distort the generous impulses of the American aid programs, has long since shown how gravely it defeats the true American interests. The Cold War has changed its character not only because Soviet policy has been evolving in response to changes in the world environment, but because the United States and its Western allies are becoming aware that anti-Communism is not an adequate response to the total situation in which we live.

# 5

# A Shift of Emphasis in Policy

INSOFAR as the United States and its allies have applied any consistent principle to their policies toward the Communist world over the past twenty years, it has been expressed in the idea of containment. The theory of containment rested upon the assumption that, if Communist expansionism could be held in check sufficiently, sooner or later changes of one sort or another would take place within the Communist system that would moderate the sources of conflict. In practice, the policy of containment was taken to mean an effort to create both general and local restraints against aggression wherever feasible, primarily by military force, but also by economic and political bulwarking. Although the climate of public support for the policy has tended from time to time to become shrill and simplistic and has contributed to an intensification of the conflict, it would seem to be a fair judgment that the policy of containment has been essentially successful and that without it the world might now have been in more difficult straits than it is. No one surely would claim that containment alone has been responsible for the changes that have been taking place in the Communist world and in the international situation, but it has at least exercised some supporting influence in the right direction, and this may be as much as one can reasonably expect any policy to do.

But none of the elements involved are static in nature— neither the Soviet system nor Soviet policies nor the background setting against which this confrontation acts itself out. Perhaps we can hope also that our understanding of the problem has become clearer with time and experience, and that we may have developed some sense of the direction in which we would like to see things move. For all these reasons, present policy requirements may be somewhat different than they were understood to be in the years immediately after the war. What seem now to be required are not radical new departures, but some shift of emphasis to take account of the fundamental characteristics of the present situation. It is mainly a matter of perspective—a way of thinking about what we are trying to do, and of clearing away the clichéd formulations that have become a substitute for thought.

If the transformations sketched in the foregoing pages are essentially correct, what are their implications for policy, on the part of the United States and, more broadly, of the West as a whole? Perhaps these can most easily be grouped into those dealing specifically with our relations with the Soviet Union and the other sectors of the Communist world, and then those that broaden the focus of our attention to problems that are complicated by, but not created by, the challenge of Communism.*

Perhaps the first thing we need to do is to rid ourselves of the "hard–soft" scale in describing policy choices, which now tends to polarize positions against an oversimplified stereotype of the problems we are dealing with. We have what might be described as a limited adversary relationship with the Soviet Union, in which the elements of continuing conflict, although extremely serious, are neither total nor absolute, being mitigated in part by the fact that our respective security interests are not wholly separable. The relationship has a dual character, and it requires of us the degree of maturity that makes it possible to be strong and firm in resisting political thrusts, prudent in the exercise of power, energetic in seeking safeguards to reduce the risk of war, and encouraging to processes of change which may moderate the underlying causes of conflict—without regarding these lines of action as contradictory, as either "hard" or "soft."

This suggests that our day-to-day decisions in meeting current crises should be shaped by an ever-present consciousness of how we would like to see the relationship move over the longer period. This is not to say that the matter is mainly in our hands to determine; but to the extent that our actions do influence Soviet developments

*Within the short scope of this chapter, it is not intended, and of course it would not be possible, to deal with all aspects of Western policy toward the Soviet Union. What I would like to do is to illustrate, by reference to a few points, the shift of emphasis from present perspectives which seems to flow from the developments analyzed in the preceding chapters.

we ought to be conscious of these consequences. Containment does produce change, but not automatically in a benign direction. In the totality of our actions and in the manner in which we do what we have to do, even in frustrating aggression, our ultimate purpose must be made evident, in order to encourage processes of change in Soviet policies and the Soviet system in the direction of moderation and responsibility.

With regard to the Soviet domestic system, while this is in the main not a matter for us to decide, neither is it a matter of indifference to us nor irrelevant to our relationship with the Soviet Union. To the extent that the present system may be less dependent upon external tensions to provide domestic cohesion, prospects for peaceful relations are improved; to the extent that checks and balances develop in Soviet decision-making, the possibility of adventurous and militant shifts of policy may be decreased. But beyond such considerations as these, we recognize that the Soviet people have the same right as we claim for ourselves to determine how they wish to organize their society without interference from abroad. Of course as individual human beings we do care about improvements in the conditions of life and of the creative spirit of the Soviet people, even where this may not be a proper concern of our government. The rivalry of nations or the competition of systems cannot smother the impulses of decency and common humanity between people.

When it comes to Soviet foreign policy, however, we can be frank to acknowledge our desire to encourage its evolution. The metamorphosis that has been described in the Soviet conception of its revolutionary aims represents in effect a process of attenuation of the revolutionary ideology which has been in many ways a major source of conflict in this relationship. We should therefore wish to encourage a further evolution in this direction, to the point where Soviet policy genuinely accepts the existence of a variety of forms of society in the world which need not be inherently hostile to each other. This need not mean the abandonment of Soviet ideas about the direction of historical change, whether Marxist or otherwise, within the framework of a mutual acceptance of an historical wager, as long as the Soviet leadership comes to recognize a self-interest in accepting orderly and nonviolent processes of change. It is *not* our purpose to defend the status quo, which would in any case be an impossible task, but it *is* our purpose to draw the Soviet Union further toward the acceptance of international processes that make possible adjustments without war.

Perhaps the best illustration of what this might imply for United States policy was the "twin option" character of the Marshall Plan proposal. Two possibilities were created, one of which would have involved Soviet participation in a mutually advantageous arrangement. The other provided for action which would go forward despite a Soviet rejection. Might there not be many fields in which such alternatives could be advanced—one of which would offer the possibility of constructive participation, while the other assured that cooperation among other nations would not be prevented by Soviet obstruction? Over a period of time—and probably a long period of time—self-interest might lead future generations of Soviet leaders to consider the advantages of limited measures of cooperation. It must be added in frankness that no one then knew what would have happened to the Marshall Plan had the Soviet Union decided the other way. No doubt it would have been beset by the same disruption and frustrations which characterized other joint Soviet-Western operations during that period. This is still the risk in any proposed common venture, but the risks can be limited and the offers must be made in good faith if the longer-term purpose is to be served.

This perspective has a corollary which concerns the difficulty of learning to operate within a framework of reduced tension, or of alternations between high and low tension. Despite the trouble we may have during periods of reduced tension in holding the alliance together, or in winning legislative support for military appropriations and foreign aid, it is clear that we cannot respond to such difficulties by an artificial regeneration of tensions. We are obliged to choose the harder course of educating our publics and our legislatures to do what needs to be done over long periods of time without the help of a crisis atmosphere.

On the other hand, this does not mean that we should exaggerate the importance of a détente in a purely "atmospheric" sense, which is sometimes used to perform tactical functions in Soviet political strategy. We should accept and even welcome a relaxation of tension where it is based upon specific measures which are in themselves useful and are related to the causes of tension. But tension is a symptom of conflicting purposes, and symbolic tension-reduction acts by themselves are at best superficial in their benefits and may lead to serious miscalculations on both sides. There has been much unnecessary mischief within the Western alliance as a result of the ambiguous meanings of the word "détente," mischief which could be reduced if the United States made clear to its continental allies that it appreciates the distinction between specific measures to reduce the danger of war and the acceptance of political compromises at their expense.

Another corollary to this approach is the further development of the largely unspoken conventions regarding the rules of conflict which have tended to emerge in practice during recent years. A certain codification of conflict seems to have developed in Europe, with each side accepting a certain freedom of political and economic maneuver within its sphere on the part of the adversary, competing for limited shifts in orientation. To some undefined extent, the understanding implies an avoidance of sudden or drastic shifts in the present gross equilibrium, or surprise deployments that may give rise to unsettling apprehensions. Less well defined have been the "Marquis of Queensberry" rules regarding intervention in conflicts in the underdeveloped areas, where conventions could usefully be extended to cover the levels of weapons and personnel to be introduced by each side into such conflict situations. The development of these rules of conflict has been largely a tacit affair, reflecting a mutual sense of responsibility and common experience, occasionally reinforced by channels of private communication. Reduction of the risk of miscalculation around crisis points, particularly, requires attention to communication between adversaries, not only in the physical transmission of messages by such devices as the "hot line," but also in the development of relationships of confidence with adversary representatives through diplomatic and if necessary extra-diplomatic channels. The great value of personal confidence in such communications, when it is possible, is likely to be more than can be publicly appreciated. This may be one of the most tangible aspects of the limited adversary relationship.

This brings us to a consideration of the implications for policy of the military threat discussed in the preceding chapter. In the early years of the Cold War, Western attention was so much centered upon Soviet military capabilities as the primary problem—the whole motivation for the formation of the Atlantic alliance stemming from the possibility of Soviet military action or pressure against Western Europe—that it is extremely difficult now to arrive at a measured judgment of the military dimension of the conflict. Differences of estimate on this point are of course deeply involved in the policy divergencies within the Western alliance. Particularly during a climate of reduced tension, it has become a prime task for Western statesmanship to arrive at a common assessment and response which is neither excessive and unnecessarily destabilizing nor inadequate for Western security and the support of Western diplomacy.

The problem arises from the effort to reconcile two somewhat conflicting considerations: the lesson of the past twenty years that adequate Western strategic power has been, and continues to be, necessary to international stability; and the real possibility of a catastrophic scale of destruction resulting from the present confrontation of Soviet and Western nuclear weapons.

These considerations require us to broaden our conception of security, in the realization that our security in the broadest sense of the word is interlocked with that of our adversary. It follows that arms control should be urgently upgraded as an integral part of Western military policy. Although there may be a high degree of rationality and even of apparent precision in the calculations of each nation regarding its military requirements, the net effect is irrational. Perhaps it is time to turn the old chestnut inside out and say that peace is too important to be left to the pacifists; those who accept the reality of force in international politics must also accept the responsibility for working toward safeguards in the military plane of our confrontation with the Soviet Union.

We are living with a false sense of confidence in the present strategic stabilization. There can be no doubt that, although this stabilization is a tenuous basis for international security, it is the best we have for the moment and is perhaps better than we might have hoped for a dozen years ago; and therefore we must regard it as a favorable development that we should welcome and wish to encourage. More than that, it should be an essential part of our purpose to study the nature of this stabilization, and to seek to underpin it as best we can against disrupting forces.

This approach to arms control is not well understood, either in the Soviet Union or among some of our allies. It should be distinguished from broad proposals for "general and complete disarmament," which would require millennial changes in the political systems and which in fact serve to block progress toward the more modest and practical safeguards at hand. Nor does this approach depend upon the illusion that the present relationship with the Soviet Union is not a relationship of serious conflict, or that our deterrent strength is anything less than vital. The present climate, which recognizes only the simple polarities of "hard" or "soft," is such that any discussion of arms control immediately arouses fears lest our will or our military security or our alliances may be weakened. On the Russian side, a deep suspicion persists that arms control conceals a Western effort to gain unilateral advantages.

What is required in the first instance is the deepening of our awareness, and of Soviet awareness, of the process of interaction by which the measures that each side takes to improve its advantage may have reciprocal effects which diminish the security of both. In this sense, optimum security is not to be equated with maximum superiority of whatever kind; qualitative judgments are required which take into account the total relationship and which work toward stability in the military field even while the political conflict may continue unabated. Approached in this spirit, it should be within the wit of man to try to identify the specific hazards that could disrupt the present deterrent balance and result in general nuclear war, and to work toward measures directed against these hazards—measures that advance neither Soviet interests nor our own in relation to the other, but that represent an area in which there does exist a parallel interest in reducing the possibility of general war.

There is less concern now than there has been in the past over the possibility that general war might be launched by surprise attack or by technical accidents or by the action of madmen, which formed the theme of several novels and motion pictures about the various ways in which World War III might originate; but there remain several other potential sources of disturbance to the balance of nuclear deterrents which are less easily dismissed.

Opinions among scientists appear to differ about the prospects for military research developments sufficiently radical to disturb the strategic balance. The prevailing view seems to be that the prospect for large scientific leaps in the near future does not appear great, but that the wider application of presently available science to military technology could—particularly under forced draft in a climate of higher tension—set off another spiral of armament effort. This could result in the comparatively near future, for example, if either side thought it even marginally profitable to intensify its work on the development of antimissile defenses.

It is of course natural that those who have professional military responsibilities on both sides should consider the technical problems of how to conduct military operations under the variety of circumstances that could conceivably arise if the deterrence system should break down; this fact in itself is inevitably a source of instability, which can be moderated only to the extent to which these considerations are subordinated to overarching political judgments as to when such contingency planning, procurement, and deployment may be more than is reasonably required, and may therefore, in its total and reciprocal effect, tend to reduce net stability.

While the political imagination rarely succeeds in

anticipating the ways in which trouble actually arises, there are several obvious sources of danger which should dictate some priorities in a major concentration of effort to develop specific and feasible arms control safeguards.

One source of potential breakdown of the deterrent system stems from the fact that force is still a fundamental element in international politics, and the use of weapons to back up diplomacy around a crisis point can easily lead to miscalculation, an incendiary accident at the point of confrontation, or loss of control of the situation. These possibilities, despite the responsibility and restraint that have characterized the behavior of the two major powers during such crises, constitute a serious risk because of the many factors that can take a situation out of control, including chance developments, lack of information, unwise decisions, or the absence of acceptable means of reducing the confrontation. Since such crises are likely to involve areas of major political interest, arms reduction agreements affecting these areas are particularly difficult to work out, although in practice some mutual restraints may prevail, such as the avoidance of sudden shifts of deployment in the area, or of the conduct of maneuvers that may be unintentionally alarming.

International security in such situations is clearly best served by aborting the crisis before it comes into being, by leaving no room for uncertainty about the respective capabilities, definition of interest, or determination. Once launched, a crisis of this kind requires unprecedentedly close coordination of political and military action. Political concessions made in the face of such duress are likely to guarantee the repetition of this kind of risk-taking. If the temptations of "adventurism" are to be resisted it must be made clear as often as necessary that these probes are not profitable, that they are costly in terms of setbacks in relation to other desired objectives, and that the inherent risks are disproportionate to any possible gain.

An equally disturbing hostage to fortune is the possible upset of the deterrent balance as a result of the action of third countries—major allies or even unallied countries which may become involved in conflicts that spiral out of control. The period of turbulence ahead in the under-developed areas seems to foreshadow a phase in international politics dominated by revolutionary upheavals whose effects upon the major powers of the industrial areas may not be easily contained, all the more so because of three particularly vexing complications: the prospect of further proliferation of nuclear weapons, the inadequacy of international procedures for managing third-area conflicts, and the Chinese exploitation of local revolutionary activity joined with the Chinese unwillingness thus far to participate in any international arms control effort.

The dangers in prospect as a result of the probable further spread of nuclear weapons clearly demand more public attention and serious government action than they are now receiving. In retrospect, we may look back upon this period as a time of lost opportunity, when decisions now being made will influence the further proliferation of nuclear weapons, decisions that could still be within our capacity to influence but may pass this point in the near future. It would be a tragic error to comfort ourselves with the counsel that this proliferation is inevitable or will not matter, and to allow the present critical period to pass without a major effort to do everything humanly possible to prevent it. Many measures have been proposed and have been considered; what is lacking is the decision to give this issue the priority it should have.

The management of third-area conflicts, like the problem of nuclear proliferation, represents a universal hazard, equally threatening to the Soviet Union and ourselves, although both problems are of course complicated by conflicting political considerations. Among the various types of conflicts that are arising in the underdeveloped world, those which the Soviet Union regards as "wars of national liberation"—which means those in which the Soviet Union has identified a major political interest— may be least susceptible to any arrangements for containing or reducing the conflict. Possibilities for the acceptance of procedures for limiting or settling local conflicts may be somewhat better in other areas where the interest in political gains is less compelling than the prospect of uncontrolled fighting, as for example in the Middle East. Once there is a mutual recognition that the dangers of uncontrolled conflict in these areas may be far greater than can be justified by the hope of political gain to anyone, it becomes feasible to consider a variety of instrumentalities at hand. These should include a reconsideration of the peacekeeping services of the United Nations, where ingenuity has by no means been exhausted in devising procedures that can be mutually acceptable, as well as ad hoc arrangements among the parties concerned to limit the flow of arms of particular categories, or of volunteers, into the area of conflict. If however the prospect of disruptive intervention by China remains, our chances of encouraging even limited cooperation on the part of the Soviet Union will not be promising. This fact has an important bearing on our policies with regard to China and the Sino-Soviet dispute, to which we will turn in a moment.

Before doing so, however, it might be well to observe that, in attempting to characterize what is implied by the term "limited adversary relationship," our emphasis has so far been upon the aspects of limitation, as a corrective to that segment of public opinion for whom life is divided into "good guys" and "bad guys." But there are also those on the other flank who persistently underestimate the depth of the political conflict involved, and who are repeatedly subject to disappointment that solutions to the Cold War cannot be found by clearing up some mis-understandings. To them it is necessary to say that the adversary side of this relationship cannot be glossed over too lightly, that it is deeply rooted in the Soviet system, and that it is no service to peace to devise solutions that do not take this fact into account.

If this essay suceeds in doing nothing else, perhaps at least it can gain some support for the conception that the two aspects of the limited adversary relationship are not mutually exclusive; both need to be kept in mind at the same time.

In the previous chapter, we observed that time and events had attenuated the force of the idea of world pro-letarian revolution in Communist ideology, and that the conflict has increasingly taken on the character of nation-state rivalry, although it is still sometimes expressed in

the language of revolution. There are many aspects to this
rivalry, ranging from performance in outer space to the
output of steel, engineers, or athletes, but the essential
character of it is to be found in the political thrust of the
Soviet Union to increase its power and influence in the
world relative to the existing distribution of power. This
thrust is based upon a Soviet analysis which is deeply
political, and upon an orchestration of a variety of means
—economic, diplomatic, cultural, etc.—to achieve political changes that will diminish the power of the Western
group of nations relative to its own power.

In considering the implications of this analysis for
Western policy, therefore, the essential point is to keep
our priorities clear. Above all, the Soviet political challenge requires primary concern for the vitality and the
integrity of the Western alliance. This is of course a much
more difficult task now than it was fifteen years ago; then,
a primitive instinct for survival sufficed against what was
understood to be an imminent military threat; now, it is a
matter of strengthening a sense of common purpose and
habits of cooperation in many fields, against a more diffuse
and ambiguous challenge and against the internal pressures of a renascent nationalism.

One reason for stressing the order of priorities is that
the revival of Western Europe and trends toward greater
autonomy in Eastern Europe have raised the question
whether the effort to integrate Eastern and Western
Europe should now take precedence over the effort to
maintain and develop the association between Western
Europe and the United States. The question as posed inter-
twines two quite different time perspectives: the prospects

for a union of East and West Europe depend upon the dissolution of fundamental characteristics in the Soviet Union and in its relations with Eastern Europe which do not appear to be likely for many years, probably many decades; while the association of Western Europe and the United States is now the heart of the power of the West, the main bulwark against Soviet pressures, and an important factor in encouraging a long-term trend toward moderation in Soviet policies.

Indeed, it would seem to be a first principle of contemporary politics that the best guarantee against a possible reversion to general militancy in Soviet foreign policy would be a continuation of the military deterrent strength of the Western alliance, and if possible a strengthening of the economic and technological base of Western power and of Western political cohesion in the face of Soviet efforts to exploit divergencies. The separation of Western Europe from the United States would weaken both, and the prospect of a future center of world power in Western Europe detached from the United States is therefore a cherished objective of Soviet political strategy. It would follow that the highest priority of Western policy should be to ensure that the rise of Western Europe to power and responsibility in the world should be accommodated within an Atlantic framework, and that the sense of community among the Atlantic nations should be strengthened by as many functional ties as possible under present circumstances. The essential character of the alliance changes of course as circumstances change; the necessity of countering the divisive thrusts of Soviet policies remains as an important, but a lesser, motivation for the alliance; what becomes of increasing significance is the need for collaboration among the industrial nations of the West toward common positive responses to problems in the world that go far beyond the Soviet challenge. This theme takes us outside the immediate problem; let us return to it later in the chapter, and stay now with the implications for the Western alliance of the present thrust of Soviet political strategy.

While recent developments do not appear to have improved the possibilities for a general settlement of European issues in the near future, the advantage of Soviet preoccupations at home and within the Communist movement is that they permit the continuation of the present ambiguous political stabilization, within which long-term trends may be encouraged without abrupt confrontations or a clear definition of relations.

In the case of Germany, the central issue of Europe, the Soviet commitment to the Eastern Zone appears to have diminished least of all its involvements in Europe, and no prospects for an early or dramatic solution to the problem of reunification appear in sight. Toward the Federal Republic, Soviet political strategy has wavered between two aims: to prevent it from attaining a dominant position in Western Europe, particularly militarily, but on the other hand to encourage within it political trends toward "independence," which is to say a lesser degree of attachment to the Western alliance. Although the reunification issue has become increasingly important in West German politics in recent years and remains a major source of instability in Europe, the encouraging fact is that the Federal Republic has remained intimately associated with the

Western alliance while growing in political experience and maturity, and has not allowed itself to become vulnerable to manipulative pressures from the East.

Particularly in the case of Eastern Europe, the present degree of ambiguous stabilization does not require either an acceptance of Soviet hegemony or a drive to produce dramatic shifts in the power relationships. What is involved is largely a matter of degree, an encouragement of autonomous trends within the limits of the present situation, such that the Soviet Union can, with grace and without feeling its vital interests threatened, accept some normalization of trade and cultural relations between Eastern Europe and the West, as well as some reduction in the severity of state controls within these states.

To delineate a policy, however, is often quite a different matter than to have it executed. Particularly is this the painful case in prescribing a policy for the Western alliance toward Eastern Europe. It is evident that a carefully modulated and differentiated policy toward Eastern Europe requires coordinated approaches to questions of trade, credits, and cultural exchanges, rather than leaving these to the interplay of competitive pressures, but it is also evident that such a unified policy is, for the present at least, an unreal expectation. Perhaps it would be more reasonable to seek to strengthen common studies of the effects of trade and cultural exchanges, so that the various policies might proceed from common assessments and, even though divergent, might be brought into some relationship with each other toward a common purpose.

The development of trade and cultural relations with the Soviet Union has on the whole been subject to ad hoc arrangements without much studied consideration being given to their effects within the Soviet Union. A certain expansion in these fields has proceeded on faith and, in the case of trade, in response to private interests. Divergent credit policies among the Western nations have been a prime political target of Soviet policy; perhaps the obverse side of this is that, given the seriousness of Soviet interest in obtaining credits for economic as well as political purposes, the need to maintain a climate of reduced tension as a condition favorable to the extension of such credits constitutes some restraint on Soviet policies. On the whole, however, it is doubtful that either trade or cultural exchanges offer any major leverage in influencing substantial changes in Soviet policy, although, in the case of the cultural exchanges, they may have poignant human significance. Both may be of considerable influence, on the other hand, in relation to Eastern Europe, provided that they are administered with some sensitivity for the differentiated conditions to be found there.

This is not the place to attempt to resolve the problems of our relations with Communist China as well, but there are certain limited aspects of these relations that are immediately relevant to our present discussion. There have been many suggestions about how the West should conduct itself in relation to the Sino-Soviet dispute. Some have urged that the West should align itself with the Soviet side of the argument, in the hope that the Soviet Union might be drawn into an alliance with the West against Chinese militancy. Others have argued that the West should conduct itself in such a way as to give indirect support to China, and thus even out the contest within the Communist world. Neither of these approaches commends itself as prudent or likely to be successful. The expectation that a Soviet-Western alliance could be forged against China grossly underestimates the ideological ties that would remain even if the Sino-Soviet dispute resulted in an open break between the two countries. The effort to strengthen the Chinese challenge to the Soviet Union runs the serious risk of encouraging reckless and militant actions that may be much more dangerous than could be justified by any possible advantage. Particularly because our instruments for any such intervention are crude and might have effects contrary to what we intend, we ought not attempt to be unduly clever about trying to manipulate the parties to this dispute against each other. Rather we should remember that we have an interest in the long-term evolution of both parties.

But while Peking is in its radical revolutionary phase of behavior, our assistance may be required in strengthening the independence of countries where there are viable governments that wish to have our help. The application of the lesson of containment to this area has been disparaged on the ground that the problem here is essentially political. This does not invalidate the conception of containment as a necessary concomitant to the long-term effort to draw China toward less militant relations with the rest of the world, but it does suggest that we must be attentive to a political analysis of the nature of the conflict in these areas, and that a combination of political, economic, and military instrumentalities may be necessary in restraining expansionism against people who wish to remain independent. An attitude of passive resignation toward this militant expansionism not only diminishes the prospect of long-term moderation of Chinese policies, but has the immediate effect of weakening trends toward restraint in Soviet policies.

This brings us to the point at which we must consider the major conclusion that emerges from the previous chapters: our relations with the Soviet Union cannot be discussed without reference to the broader context of international politics today. Indeed, the central problem for the United States or the West is not the Soviet Union, which is another way of saying that the Cold War is not the all-embracing issue in international politics. The Soviet Union is a serious complicating factor in a time in which the main characteristics are the strengthening of tendencies toward nationalism, violence, and international anarchy. The central problem is how to survive this period without general war, and how to influence the direction of events toward the strengthening of international processes which can accommodate change without violence.

The problem of dealing with local manifestations of Communism in the underdeveloped areas is inseparable from the problem of the widening gap between the industrialized and the underdeveloped parts of the world. The only effective kind of anti-Communism in these areas is that which, like an antibiotic, inhibits the growth of a microorganism by destroying the nutrients on which it feeds.

In association with our allies—for this is their problem as much as it is ours, whether they are ready to recognize this responsibility or not—we should address ourselves to the necessity of providing a democratic alternative to the totalitarian model of development in Asia, Africa, and Latin America, and of encouraging the forces of nationalism in these areas to find their expression, not in identification with Communism and not in demagogic violence, but in the tradition of a constructive and integrative nationalism. This is the most potent source of political energy in the world today, and it should be channeled into the drive to discover what modernization should mean for each people on its own terms.

It is relevant to remind ourselves here that the West has a persistent and fundamental interest, in the background at all times, in encouraging the growth and acceptance of an international system among the nation-states—"system" here not necessarily meaning a particular institutional form, but more broadly referring to the deepening of habits of cooperation and restraint, the strengthening of accepted procedures for managing change and limiting conflict. This is why we must have an interest in the process as well as the substance of the resolution of international problems. That this is a central part of our purpose gives added importance to the "how" of doing things, in order that the manner of our conduct shall have the effect of strengthening the patterns of international behavior we would wish to see prevail. No advice can be more pernicious than that we should "fight fire with fire"—to contribute to the degradation of international conduct because of the jungle ethics of an adversary.

The United Nations now has the possibility of becoming a universal institution, but it is in a phase of growth in which it is absorbing a greatly enlarged constituency. As with any living political organism, it must rediscover in experience how it must function under changed circumstances, and this will take time, and faith. Its purposes meanwhile must be supported by a host of instrumentalities.

Among these, a central responsibility devolves upon the Atlantic group of nations. Perhaps the most important rationale for the closer association of this group today is to be found in the fact that among their shared values is a common interest in strengthening international habits of cooperation. In the present period, their sense of community can best be expressed, not through large institutional innovations, but through myriad forms of consultation, planning, cooperative action, and division of labor on problems everywhere in the world which are, or ought to be, as much a matter of concern to our allies as they are to us. What is required, however, is that we should define our national interests in terms of sufficient breadth and vision that they will have relevance for people in all countries who are our natural allies.

The shift of emphasis in policy that is required must begin with the recognition that the Cold War—as a term, and as a conception—does not provide an adequate framework for thinking about the kinds of problems that need our attention. Not that the Cold War is over, but it has been transformed and merged into a larger and more complex setting.

What lies beyond the Cold War, then? No surcease of

conflict, surely, nor some alternative slogan, but an urgent
and tangled array of challenges to international order
which defy any simplified catch-phrase. It may be that
there is a public need for a few schematic notions to make
the complexities of foreign affairs fit into a comprehen-
sible pattern, but the guiding popular conceptions must
be made more adequate to the situation that exists. Even
the wisest of policies cannot be effective if public support
has to be won for them by the manipulation of outworn
and oversimplified themes. The public should share in
the difficult revision of thought which experience has been
forcing on the decision-makers.

It is not utopian, I believe, to expect public acceptance
for the notion that our relations with the Soviet Union
are and should be multidimensional in order that we may
oppose where necessary and collaborate where possible,
having always in mind a longer-term sense of direction
toward the moderation of conflict.

Even in the containment of Chinese power, which now
begins to preoccupy us, the lesson of past experience with
the Soviet Union would be lost if we did not understand
and respond to the sources of conflict which go far beyond
Communism. Our perspectives must be broad enough to
encompass the period of violent transitions into which
we are moving, in which the varied forms of Communism
are understood as complicating factors entwined among
the many sources of conflict to which our attention must
also be directed.

And in responding to these immediate needs, we must
give greater emphasis than we have to process as well as
purpose, in order that our actions will strengthen the

habits and institutions of international cooperation and deepen the restraints on the use of force which are essential to the kind of environment in which free societies can survive and flourish. It is this sense of the direction toward which we would like to see things move that should be reflected in everything we do, as well as in what we say.